Felicity Goodyear-Smith is a family doctor who has worked in the sexual abuse field since 1982. As a police doctor specialising in sexual assault examinations, she helped set up many of the procedures for the medical examination of rape and sexual abuse victims in New Zealand. She was a founding member and chairperson of the HELP Foundation Trust, an organisation which provides counselling and medical care to all sexual assault victims.

In 1992, while she was General Practitioner for the Centrepoint Community, two women and seven men, including her husband and her parents-in-law, were imprisoned for sexual abuse.

Her unique situation of extensive work in the field, coupled with experience of the system "from the other side", gives her an exceptional understanding and appreciation of the issues.

Also by Felicity Goodyear-Smith:
Sexual Assault Examinations — A Guide for Medical Practitioners
(with Margaret Lawton & Peta Stringer)

*To my husband
and other friends*

ISBN 0-86470-047-4

Copyright © Felicity Goodyear Smith 1993
First published 1993

All rights reserved. This book is copyright and no part may be published in any form whatsoever without prior permission, in writing, from Benton-Guy Publishing Ltd, Box 46-018, Auckland, New Zealand. Tel. (09) 360-3281, Fax (09) 360-2180.

Cover design by Paul Woodruffe
Printed by Chameleon

FIRST DO NO HARM

THE SEXUAL ABUSE INDUSTRY

FELICITY GOODYEAR-SMITH
MB ChB DipObst MRNZCGP

Benton-Guy Publishing
Box 46-018, Auckland, New Zealand

৫৷

Table of contents

Acknowledgments 4
Foreword 5
Chapter 1: The Politics Of Sexuality 14
    The subjective nature of reality 15
    Sexuality as a social construct 18
    The politics of sexuality 19
    Cycles in beliefs and attitudes 22
    Moral panics and social scapegoats 24
Chapter 2: Sex In The 20th Century 27
    Women's role in a pre-technological world 27
    Emancipation of women in the twentieth century 27
    The anti-sex movement of the 1980s and 1990s 28
    Modern feminist analysis 30
    Return of the double standard 30
    The ideology of victimology 31
Chapter 3: Growth of the Sexual Abuse Industry 33
    The history of child sexual abuse 33
    Development of the sexual abuse field in the last two decades ... 34
    Faulty assumptions underpinning the field 35
    Lack of professional and ethical scrutiny 36
    Victimology and the sexual abuse industry 38
    The conflict between the evidence-gathering and treatment roles of workers 38
Chapter 4: Can memories always be believed and trusted? ... 40
    Issues of suggestibility and the accuracy of memory ... 41
    Influences that distort memory 42
        Time 42
        Post-event misinformation 42
        Distortions as a result of interviewer expectations ... 43
        Thinking, writing about and discussing a memory 44
        Sharing memories with other participants 44
        Dream or fantasy with memories of real events 45
        Current beliefs and feelings 46
    Effects of interviewing techniques on memory 46
    Recall under counselling and hypnosis 50
    Accuracy of clinical judgements and predictions 51

First do no Harm

    The effect of stress on witness accuracy 52
    Credibility in the courtroom 52
Chapter 5: What is sexual abuse? 54
    Legal definitions 55
    Social definitions 56
    Sociological definitions 58
    Retrospective definitions 58
    Definition difficulties.. 59
    Interpretation of statistics 61
Chapter 6: Childhood sexuality 64
    Historical review of adult/child sex 64
    Anthropological studies... 64
    Sexuality of children 68
    Children's sexual rights 70
    Secondary victimisation and iatrogenic abuse 73
    Child sex offenders 73
Chapter 7: Some specific directions the sexual abuse industry is taking us 75
    Child day-care cases 76
        The Virginia McMartin Preschool, California. 77
        Country Walk Babysitting Service, Florida. 78
        The Wee Care Day Nursery, New Jersey. 80
        Civic Daycare Centre, Christchurch. 82
    Satanic ritual abuse 83
        Jordan, Minnesota. 83
        Oude Pekela, the Netherlands. 84
        Orkney Islands. 85
        Rochdale, Manchester 85
    Alternative communities 86
        Children of God, Australia. 87
        Centrepoint Community, Auckland, New Zealand. 88
        Branch Davidians, Waco, Texas. 91
        Cooperite sect, South Island, New Zealand. 91
    Child pornography 92
Chapter 8: False complaints 96
    Custody cases 97
    Teenage retribution 102
    Pressure from peers, parents, and people in authority 103
    Emotional payoff in being a victim 104
    Financial gains 105
Chapter 9: The industry's contribution to the sexual abuse epidemic 107

Mandatory reporting	108
Hotlines	109
Political motivations and religious agendas	110
Child sexual abuse accommodation syndrome	111
Multiple personalities	112
Munchausen Syndrome by Proxy	114
Faulty medical indicators of abuse	115

Chapter 10: Implications and consequences of the sexual abuse industry beliefs 119

Effects of networking	119
Effects of prevention programmes	120
Persecution of professionals who challenge the industry	122
Sex offender registries	123
Social implications	125
The backlash movement	125

Chapter 11: Victims rule OK? Victimocracy and alternative philosophies. 127

General world trend of victimology	128
Male oppressor/female victim	130
Forgiveness, compassion and love	131
Alternative model of female/male relationships	134

Appendix: Ways the problems can be redressed 138

Research	138
Education	139
Diagnosis of sexual abuse	140
Medical procedures	141
Police procedures	141
Courtroom practices	141
Treatment of sexual abuse victims	142
Treatment of offenders	143
Legal considerations	144
The Media	144

References 146
Name Index 161
Subject Index 165

Acknowledgments

I acknowledge the considerable support and assistance I have received in writing this book. I am truly grateful to all those loving friends who have stood by me and sustained me.

It is impossible for me to name everyone but I wish to particularly acknowledge and thank the following:

Larry Constantine for inspiring me and for providing me with invaluable written material and overseas contacts.

The members of Parents Against Injustice (PAIN) and others who shared their stories with me. and gave me copies of their transcripts and other case material.

Peter Fitzsimons for helping me learn how to drive my computer.

David Woodward for his dedicated editorial assistance.

Bill Taylor for helping me get it published.

And most of all my husband, John Potter, both for his contributions to the text and for his loving support.

Foreword

This book is about the development of the sexual abuse industry in the Western world in the last decade. My basic assertion is that there are some very faulty premises at the core of this field, and that these are having far-reaching and tragic consequences. While I do wish to draw public attention to the way in which some of these terrible mistakes are being made, I do not in any way mean to deny nor negate all the helpful and valuable assistance given to genuine sexual abuse victims by workers in this area. It is however vital that our ways of dealing with the problem come under close scrutiny, to ensure that our responses do good and not harm.

I am aware that my critics will accuse me of presenting only one side of the argument. I make no apologies about this however. We are bombarded daily with the opposite viewpoint, on television and from our newsstands. Our bookshops are stocked with a proliferation of volumes about sexual abuse, but you would be hard-pressed to find one which questions current beliefs about the nature and prevalence of sexual abuse.

Everywhere we look these days, we are inundated with messages which put forward what I believe are myths and erroneous assumptions about sexual abuse. This is not to say that sexual abuse does not occur, but genuine cases are being swamped by what is being perceived as a sexual abuse epidemic. I contend that much of this is actually being created by the machinery of the sexual abuse industry, which is fuelled by personal moral and political beliefs and by public outrage and hysteria.

The arguments presented in this book offer what I believe is a scientific and rational perspective backed by substantial studies and research. Much of what I discuss is counter to the mainstream beliefs about sexual abuse disseminated in our society. One of my chief concerns about the sexual abuse industry is that it is not open to challenge: there is only orthodoxy or heresy.

I was one of the pioneers in this field. I am now viewed as a traitor to the cause. My years of professional experience are strangely juxtaposed with the unexpected personal circumstances in which I have subsequently found myself. As my story will show, I have close connections with some of the cases described in this book. There are some who will say that such involvement will have coloured my perceptions and should disqualify me from writing such a book.

Indeed, such considerations, coupled with threats to my professional registration and hence my livelihood, have stopped me from speaking out for several years. However, my concerns about what has happened and continues to happen have reached a point where I can no longer remain silent. The detailed case studies and research papers I have accumulated over the years gives me a knowledge and understanding of the issues available to few others, and I believe it is important for me to share this publicly.

What I have to say in this book is backed by a substantial body of reputable literature. I ask the reader to evaluate what I discuss on this basis. I know there are those who will try to use my personal associations and connections to discredit me and invalidate my assertions. My request is that you read this book with an open mind and judge the material it contains on its own merits.

I have written this book with the lay reader in mind. I believe it will be invaluable reading for anyone who has been involved or associated with false allegations of abuse, who is concerned about the apparent sexual abuse epidemic, or who is worried about the increasing state intervention in private and family lives.

This book could also be used as a important resource for anyone working in the sexual abuse field. Because this is such a multi-disciplinary field, this includes doctors and other health professionals, psychologists, counsellors and therapists, social workers, police, workers within the justice system and educators at all levels.

It will be of interest to parents and child care workers who are becoming afraid to cuddle and comfort children for fear their actions be misinterpreted.

This book is the result of both my professional experiences and my private circumstances. I therefore feel it is necessary for me to share the significant events in my life which have led to my writing it.

I first become involved in sexual abuse work in 1982. At that time, I was a full-time General Practitioner in inner city Auckland, New Zealand. A sexual assault centre (named HELP) was being set up in conjunction with the police to counsel and medically examine rape victims. I organised specialist training in this field for myself and four other women doctors. We were appointed as Police Medical Officers and were available on a rostered basis for all cases of sexual assault in our region, working in conjunction with the HELP centre.

The following year I accepted an invitation to serve as a Trustee of the HELP Foundation, and was subsequently appointed the Chair of the Trust. I therefore became involved in the administration and the politics of the organisation, as well as having clinical duties to perform. My involvement in the field later extended to teaching doctors and other health professionals about various aspects of sexual assault management. I was appointed honorary Medical Officer at Auckland's children's hospital for the purpose of performing sexual abuse examinations. I published several papers and wrote a sexual assault examination guide for medical practitioners in conjunction with forensic scientists working in the field (Lawton, Goodyear and Stringer, 1987). I also presented papers on various sexual assault issues at several international conferences.

Although HELP was initially set up to provide care for women victims of rape, we soon began seeing large numbers of children with alleged sexual abuse. When we first started doing this work, women who complained of rape and children who claimed sexual abuse were likely to be disbelieved. HELP provided a safe caring environment for them to tell their stories, and receive support and assistance. Our services included medical and counselling care, and aid with any ensuing police and court proceedings. In fact, we often had two very distinct roles: one was forensic (gathering of legal evidence), the other therapeutic.

Over the next few years, the number of cases seen at the Centre multiplied. Some of these were acute rapes, but the majority of new cases were due either to cases of alleged child abuse or to adult women claiming sexual molestation some time in the past.

The organisation began to attract women with strong political beliefs. Rape and sexual abuse were increasingly thought of among staff as abuses of male power in a patriarchal society. Protocols were developed to ensure the Centre was "politically correct" with respect to feminist, racial and sexual orientation issues. The only real way of preventing abuse was seen to be changing society. For some of the women associated with HELP, redressing political concerns was seen as more important than working with individual clients.

I began to have increasing concerns about some of the cases we were seeing and the effects of intervention. I saw some cases where allegations were clearly false. In particular, I witnessed some terrible situations where children were pawns in custody battles. I became aware of how easily children's stories can be distorted or created by the interview process. I saw how children may learn what the examiner wants in an interrogation, and come to believe that abuse happened to them when it hadn't.

I became worried about the effects of what I saw as over-intervention and false allegations. I found it very difficult to talk about these matters with my colleagues, some of whom tended to label any dissension as the "backlash".

I agreed that the problem could be seen as a symptom of a hierarchical and patriarchal society, but I could also see that women could get bogged down in blaming men for this. Claiming their anger was obviously an important first step in taking responsibility for themselves, but there was nowhere obvious to go beyond that, and often they got trapped in bitterness and hostility towards men. I could see no way that men could do it "right".

Likewise, there was no way I could do it "right" for all the conflicting issues. In particular, trying to be "politically correct" with respect to feminist, racial and sexual orientation issues often meant that what happened was not necessarily in the best interest of our individual clients. For example, the HELP protocol specified that where-ever possible, counsellors should be matched by race and gender to their clients, and in many instances, this did in fact suit our clients well. However, sometimes it was totally inappropriate. For example, most Polynesian communities in Auckland are small and close-knit. For a young Samoan woman who has just been raped or revealed incest in her family, the last person she may want to confide in is a member of her own community. Likewise, I believe that in some instances it may be beneficial or even preferable for a woman who has been raped to be counselled by a man.

Eventually I did it right for myself and resigned from the HELP Trust in 1986. By this time I was worried about the whole public outcry around sexual abuse. I did not believe that children were lying about sexual abuse, but saw that the actual interrogation techniques might be distorting the truth. I was also getting increasingly concerned that what actually constituted sexual abuse was not being clearly defined, and that the interpretation was getting broader and broader.

Soon after this I met my husband, John. He had spent seven years of his adult life living in an intentional community where his father, Bert Potter, was the spiritual leader. John had joined the community, named Centrepoint, at its inception in 1978. He had resigned his membership in 1985 and had been living away from the community for a year when I came to know him.

Centrepoint was set up as a therapeutic community which encouraged intimacy between its members.[1] Its primary aim could be defined as experiencing unconditional loving of oneself, and hence of others. There was a commitment by members to clear their resentments with others and not to hold onto feelings of hostility and bitterness. Adults were expected to take full responsibility for their feelings and behaviour and not wallow in self-destructive blame (of either themselves or others) or guilt.

The founding members of Centrepoint were mostly families of successful professional people in their thirties. They were doctors, nurses, teachers and therapists who were seeking something more in life than was available in their nuclear family suburban lives. The shared extended family life at Centrepoint offered intimacy, adventure, and a spiritual dimension to their lives which they perceived as previously lacking.

Intimacy included sexual intimacy. Sexuality was viewed as something to be enjoyed and celebrated and open relationships were advocated. Started during the

---

1. *Although I had first met John's father, Bert Potter, in the early 1970s, I was living overseas when Centrepoint was started, and I had no contact with the community during its early years. My involvement dates from mid-1988, when we became their close neighbours. My knowledge of what occurred there in its first few years is therefore gleaned from information I have read and heard about from the original members.*

permissive era of the 1970s, Centrepoint was certainly the scene of considerable sexual experimentation in its first few years. Such experimentation waned as the community matured and public awareness of sexual abuse issues started to surface in the early 1980s.

Consistent with the model of open sexuality, it was believed that children should be given positive messages about sex. Adult contacts were not hidden from children. Although initiation of sexual contact with children by adults was never condoned, some children and adolescents were not discouraged when they demonstrated an interest in sexual activities. Some parents actually encouraged their children to be sexually active. There were several teenage girls who would initiate contact with adult men, and some formed ongoing relationships whilst under the age of consent.

For the founding adults, those were challenging days, with new ways of relating to explore, community businesses to establish, and community buildings to erect. Some of their children, however, were unhappy with the move from their secure nuclear homes to Centrepoint, but had no choice in the matter. Although they may also have enjoyed the freedom and fun it gave them, some found themselves relatively neglected by parents who were caught up in the excitement and drama of founding this radically new community. For some, especially a few of the young teenage girls, being openly sexually active gave them the parental attention and approval they sought.

I believe it was unhealthy and inappropriate for young people to explore their sexuality in this way and for these reasons.

This became increasingly recognised by the community as it matured. By 1982, it appears this sort of behaviour had virtually ceased, and whilst children and adolescents would often still be exploring their sexuality, it would nearly if not always be amongst their peers.

When I met John in 1986, I realised how "burnt out " I was from my work in the sexual abuse field, added to the demands of full-time General Practice. I realised that the challenge had gone from my General Practice work; and that now was the time for me, for relationships and family.

The following year I resigned from the sexual assault roster, sold my General Practice, and travelled overseas with John.

Upon our return in January 1988, we were met with the distressing news that all my savings, including the proceeds from the sale of my practice, had been unwisely invested by my accountant in our absence, and he had lost my money in the 1987 stock-market crash.

John's two sons from his first marriage lived with their mother and her new partner in Albany not far from the Centrepoint community. We wished to live nearby and share child-care. I owned a house in the city which we could eventually sell after sorting out some legal complications. Our interim solution was to purchase a mobile home and find somewhere in Albany to locate it.

After looking around the district, we came to an arrangement with Centrepoint to move our home onto their land, about a kilometre from where the Community was sited. There we lived as an autonomous family, quite separate from the Community down the hill, for several years until our affairs were sorted out and we could buy land nearby and build our house.

I was awarded a grant from the New Zealand Medical Research Council, and spent 1988 conducting and writing up some research in the sexual abuse field. I also continued my employment in medical consultancy in a city clinic where I had been working intermittently since the early 1980s.

Centrepoint's medical needs were provided by a resident doctor, who had a small surgery set up there. He was elderly and wished to retire. In 1989 at his request I took over his job as Centrepoint doctor and ran regular clinics for the community residents.

I had heard stories from my husband John and other founding members of Centrepoint about the early days and knew that there had been inappropriate sexual activities involving children. For my own reassurance, I needed to find out whether this behaviour was still occurring. With my knowledge and experience in the sexual abuse field, I was obviously particularly alert to this possibility in my patients.

Observation of the children and conversations with the adults relieved my mind. There seemed no indication that adults were sexually exploiting the children.[2] The resident children were sexualised to the extent that seeing naked adults and witnessing sexual activity between adults was a normal part of their lives. Many of the pre-schoolers would indulge in sex-play with each other, and some of the under-age teenagers were sexually active with their peers, but not to any greater extent than adolescents in any society I have worked in.

I ran an educational programme on sexual abuse for the Community. This included a workshop and written material in the Centrepoint magazine. I also ran teenage meetings on sexual issues. I was reassured that those who were sexually active were so from choice, and did not feel that they were under any coercion. They were also exceptionally well-informed and responsible regarding contraception and prevention of sexually transmitted diseases.

It is common in intentional communities, especially those headed by charismatic leaders, that members who leave, especially those who have been devout followers, become the community's most ardent critics. Centrepoint is no exception.[3] In the

---

2. A year or two later an active paedophile was in fact identified within Centrepoint. The Community asked him to leave. They arranged for him to attend counselling with the local social services, but decided not to press charges as it was felt that such action would help neither him nor the children involved.
3. Allegations against the Centrepoint Community are also covered in greater depth in the section Alternative communities *in Chapter 7 and the section* Pressure from peers, parents and people in authority *in Chapter 8.*

late 1980s, several former members, some now working in the sexual abuse field, began speaking out against Centrepoint and its leader, Bert Potter.

Matters came to a head in 1989, when a man living outside the community attempted to gain custody of his daughter who was living there with her mother, by alleging that she was being sexually abused. One of the ex-members took up his cause, providing an affidavit for the court supporting his accusations on the grounds that sexual abuse had occurred at Centrepoint and was still happening. He also contacted other ex-residents and asked if they would provide the court with similar statements.

I assessed the child, and found no evidence to support the claims of molestation. A family court hearing decided the child was not at risk and awarded joint custody. My stand in the case became known and a number of professionals came to understand that I had colluded with sexual abuse. I know of at least one public meeting where it was stated that I should be deregistered.[4]

Contact was established between many of the young people who had lived at Centrepoint as children or adolescents in the first few years. Sexual experiences they had had before the age of consent were now maintained to have been sexual abuse.

A group of young people now began to identify themselves as victims of sexual abuse at Centrepoint (although some of those who had had sexual experiences with adults during that era refused to define themselves in this way). They obtained government-funded counselling and a number of them were awarded lump-sum compensation payments for the permanent damage they had suffered. They met together on a number of occasions, sometimes socially and sometimes in a therapy group. A police officer was present for at least one meeting. The police encouraged the women to lay charges against some of the men they had been sexually involved with. Some of the women stated that they had not realised they had been sexually abused until they talked about it with each other and attended counselling.

When I heard about what was happening, I contacted some of the ex-members involved by letter and in person, to see if dialogue and meeting between all those involved could help heal what I saw as a more and more damaging situation. My attempts were met with hostility. Several other people tried with similar response. The identity of the complainants was confidential. Some of the young women now felt that a decade ago they had been terribly damaged by people whom until recently they had treated as friends. The complainants said they wanted to lay charges against these people to prevent children currently living in the Community from being molested. It was claimed that sexual abuse was still happening at Centrepoint, but again neither victims nor offenders were named.

I knew that most of those accused felt very sorry that these young women now felt this way. I believed that facilitated sessions between all concerned were more likely

---

4. My "blacklisting" and the threats to my deregistration are also discussed in the section Persecution of professionals who challenge the industry *in Chapter 10.*

to be healing than legal actions. I met with the reaction that it was totally inappropriate for me to suggest that victims should face their offenders.

The situation dictated that people take sides. There was much rushing to the moral high ground by many who had been involved in the early sexual experimentation. Some claimed that they had been under Bert's power at the time and were not responsible for their behaviour. Some parents who had previously encouraged their adolescents to be sexually active now supported their claims that they had been permanently damaged by their experiences, and that the adults involved were to blame.

Eventually five women laid charges against eleven men and two women. None of the parents of the victims were charged. Those indicted were mostly key members of Centrepoint, and included my husband John, my mother-in-law Margie, and of course my father-in-law, Bert Potter.[5]

There were many factors operating which frequently cause memories to be inaccurate or unreliable. These include the passage of time between the event and the recall (a decade or more), the recovering of memories through therapy, discussing them with others and writing about them (see Chapter 4). Whilst there is no doubt that some of the incidents claimed did happen, the possibility of their memories being contaminated should be considered, and it is impossible to ascertain today what did or did not happen so long ago. The trials took place in 1991 and 1992. The outcome of these is described in the section on Centrepoint Community in Chapter 7.

New Zealand has very few expert witnesses prepared to testify in court on how memory can be distorted and contaminated. Such evidence is likely to attract the wrath of most professionals who work with sexual abuse, who claim that complainants' stories are always "the truth" and that offenders will always lie and deny. Professionals challenging this claim are likely to be accused of collusion with abuse.

Some of the ex-members assisting the police were concerned that I would appear as an expert witness for the defence. In fact, I had no intention of doing so, as I was so closely related to some of the accused. They accused me of having perjured myself in the evidence I had given in Bert Potter's drug trial in March 1990, and one of them contacted the police, suggesting they charge me. Another of the witnesses later admitted in court that he wanted to destroy my reputation and mana in the sexual abuse field, to ensure I would not testify in the trials. I was arrested in a dawn raid by six policemen at our home in April 1992. My computer was seized at that time by the police, who examined and made copies of all my sexual abuse writings.

My trial took place in July 1993. After the prosecution had presented their case, the judge ruled that, even if he took all their evidence at face value, the charge was not proved, and I was acquitted.

As my concerns about the sexual abuse field have mounted over the past few years,

---

5. *By this time, Bert was already in prison on drugs-related charges.*

my opinions have begun to be known. I have found myself sought out by a number of people who have suffered some of the devastating consequences of false allegations. I have in my possession a growing number of files documenting these cases. Over the past few years I have also corresponded with a number of professionals overseas who share my disquiet. They have provided me with a wealth of research papers and other material not generally available in this country. Added to this are papers and books I have accessed using computer data bases.

Although most of what I say in this book is available in these various sources, most of these each tell only a small part of the story. For several years I have wanted to put all this material together and make it publicly available. My association with Centrepoint and close relationships with "convicted child molesters", coupled with serious attempts to have me discredited and deregistered, has stopped me speaking out until now.

My critics will undoubtedly declare that I am biased. From my perspective however, my unique situation of extensive work in the field, coupled with my experiences of the system "from the other side", gives me an exceptional understanding and appreciation of the issues.

As a clinician, my primary allegiance is to my patient. One of my main concerns in the sexual abuse field is that for many workers, trying to change society comes before individual client care.

My training as a doctor has taught me to respect the scientific method in testing a theory or treatment. A new drug might appear to have exciting possibilities as a wonder-cure. Careful trials must be run, however, to determine its actual effectiveness and the possibility of harmful side-effects. Wherever possible, we must avoid disasters such as the Thalidomide tragedy, where a drug used to settle nausea in pregnancy resulted in the birth of a large number of seriously deformed babies.

We must also beware pseudoscience, where opinions and theories masquerade as proven facts without the testing required to validate them.

It is my contention that the sexual abuse industry operates on a number of untested premises and assumptions with regard to diagnosis and treatment of abuse. The ill-effects of some of these are having far-reaching and tragic consequences. I believe that these investigation and management protocols should be subject to the same evaluation as any medical therapy. Whenever any intervention is contemplated, the primary consideration should always be that which forms the basis of the Hippocratic oath: **first do no harm.**

1. The Politics of Sexuality

"CHILD SEX RING SHOCK"
Sunday News, 2 Aug 1992.

"ISLAND CHILDREN TELL OF SEX ORDEAL
WITH HOODED MAN"
The Daily Telegraph, 28 Aug 1991.

"SECT ACCUSED OF ABUSING CHILDREN: COURT HEARS
ALLEGATIONS OF SEXUAL RELATIONS WITH ADULTS
AND PROSTITUTION"
The Australian, 19 May 1992.

"THE LAST TABOO: NURSERY CRIMES"
The Bulletin, 20 Aug 1991.

"ONE IN FOUR NEW ZEALAND GIRLS ARE SEXUALLY
ABUSED BEFORE THEY TURN 18"
NZ Listener, 13 Aug 1988.

Every day we are bombarded by messages such as these proclaiming the horrors befalling our children. Western civilisation, at least in English-speaking countries, appears to be in the midst of a vast sexual abuse epidemic. In the last decade governments have spent enormous sums of money in this area, with no apparent effect in reducing the abuse. The nature and extent of the problem seems to be growing ever worse. How has this come about? What can be done about it?

This book looks at the way this situation has developed, and the factors which contribute to this perceived epidemic. It explores what is being defined as abusive. It looks at how genuine child abuse gets confused with false allegations and suggests that much of the current abuse is inadvertently created by the actions of a growing sexual abuse industry.

There is a growing awareness internationally, particularly amongst doctors, psychologists and researchers in academic circles, that the current teachings of the sexual abuse field are based on some faulty, non-scientific assumptions. Most of their writing is simply dismissed by the sexual abuse industry as part of the "backlash" against feminism. This information is therefore not disseminated in the reading lists and teaching of sexual abuse workers.

It is hard to discover exactly what is happening to our children in their homes, their schools and within our social systems. There are obviously many confounding issues contributing to the overall picture. Whatever the causes, large-scale sexual abuse of children is our contemporary social reality.

The subjective nature of reality

Until recently, most human beings were born into specific cultures and religions. They were largely exposed to only one set of beliefs, attitudes and values and they had very little opportunity for choosing a different world view from the one they were born into. The rare individuals who challenged the beliefs of their times risked at least ostracism, at worst charges of heresy or treason, usually punishable by death.

Contact with other groups or nations with different political or religious beliefs could cause unbearable conflict. Many battles and wars were fought because one race or nation could not tolerate another holding a different world view. Each would try to convert the other, or destroy it. History is full of instances where conquerors imposed their religious beliefs and social structures on defeated peoples. The Mogul invasion of India, the Moors in Spain, the Christian conversion by the British Empire of indigenous people, including the New Zealand Maori, the Communist regime of Eastern Europe, are a few of numerous examples.

Religious wars persist today. Catholic Croats, Orthodox Christian Serbs and Muslims are currently slaughtering each other in former Yugoslavia. Ireland's peace is a fragile one.

The tendency in the modern world, however, is for societies to be pluralistic. Most people are exposed through travel and communications technology to many different ways of seeing the world. People do not always remain with the religion and culture they are born into. Many adults choose their faith and the society they live in.

Once they understand that our ideas about human reality are social constructs, people become freer to move between them. Different groups of people construct different realities. There is no absolute truth - though a number of groups do claim to possess it. Religions, political ideologies and scientific theories are all symbols of meaning, and shape the ways we see the world. Each one, like a coloured glass filter, makes it easier for us to see some things and harder to see others.

By looking at our own beliefs, we are able to change them and take on new values or ways of seeing the world. We can, however, only replace one belief system with another. Our beliefs determine our social interactions. Human beings can never be free of all beliefs (Anderson, 1991).

Belief systems are based on models. Too often, however, people using models fail to recognise them as such, and hence do not see their limitations. No paradigm can explain all the facts, and once serious anomalies are encountered, a new construct needs to be found.

A good example of this is the experience of Galileo, in the early seventeenth century. From the interpretation of his telescopic observations of the night sky, Galileo challenged the belief that the earth was the centre of the universe. He supported the theory of Copernicus that the earth and planets revolve on their own axes and move in orbit around the sun.

Now, belief systems, especially those which are widely held, are extremely resistant to change. Holding and expounding this view was considered to be heresy by the Inquisition, and Galileo was forced to repudiate his theory. It is only now, nearly four hundred years later, that the Catholic church is admitting they were wrong and are considering pardoning him.

There have always been visionaries who have recognised that we create our own realities. Two thousand five hundred years ago, Buddha taught of the illusionary nature of human experience. Plato wrote that we are like people in a cave seeing only the shadows thrown on the wall by the fire. The Jewish faith abounds with stories indicating the multiple nature of reality. Indeed, it is said that in a room containing twelve Jews, there will be thirteen opinions.

There is a story told in the Sayings of the Fathers, 6:5, that demonstrates very clearly how we create our own realities:

> *There was a rabbi who wanted to see both Heaven and Hell. And God who has hidden from us the opposites and their unity, gave way to his pleading.*
>
> *The rabbi found himself before a door, which bore no name. He trembled as he saw it open before him. It gave into a room, and all was prepared for a feast. There was a table, and at its centre a great dish of steaming food. The smell and the aroma inflamed the appetite. The diners sat around the table with great spoons in their hands, yet they were shrieking with hunger, and fainting with thirst in that terrible place. They tried to feed themselves, and gave up, cursing God the author and origin of their torment. For the spoons God had provided were so long that they could not reach their faces and get the food to their tongues. They stretched out their arms, but their mouths remained empty. So they starved because of these spoons while the dish of plenty lay amongst them. And the rabbi knew their shriekings were the cries of Hell. And as knowledge came, the door closed before him.*

He shut his eyes in prayer, and begged God to take him away from that terrible place. When he opened them again, he despaired, for the same door stood before him, the door that bore no name. Again it opened, and it gave onto the same room. Nothing had changed, and he was about to cry in horror. There was the table, and at its centre the steaming bowl, and around it were the same people, and in their hands the same spoons.

Yet the shrieking had gone, and the cries and the curses had changed to blessings. And nothing had changed, yet everything. For with the same long spoons they reached to each other's faces, and fed each other's mouths. And they gave thanks to God the author and origin of their joy.

And as the rabbi heard the blessings, the door closed. He bent down, and he too blessed God who had shown him the nature of Heaven and Hell, and the chasm - a hairsbreadth wide - that divides them.

Faith and reason have increasingly been seen to be in conflict. Seventeenth century French philosopher, physicist and mathematician Rene Descartes has had an important impact on world thinking for the last three centuries. Descartes believed that everything in the universe could be reduced to space, matter, and motion, and operated under mathematical laws. This formed the basis of scientific reasoning.

In the ensuing years, science has replaced religion as the absolute truth. Science is supposed to be unbiased, disinterested, balanced and unemotional, an observation of what is. Modern-day scientists still acknowledge the usefulness and power of the scientific method but now also recognise its limitations.

It is now seen that unbiased observation is not possible. What is actually observed in a scientific study is not nature itself but the interplay between nature and the observer. Matter, events and behaviour are all changed in the act of observing and recording them.

Science can prove a hypothesis is false but never prove that it is true. It looks for the best fit of data to a theory, but not an exact match. As such, it is a valid tool for processing information, but not the total answer to the nature of reality. Any school of thought which claims to be in possession of the absolute truth in any field is in fact a closed belief system and not scientific.

Revolutionary writers such as Karl Marx and deconstructionalists such as Michel Foucault have examined the social, political and economic forces which have created modern moral beliefs. They recognise that power grabs and conspiracies often shape the social definitions of reality.

Studies have shown that the left side of our brains make up stories to explain events (Anderson 1991). For example, a scientist did an experiment with a young boy whose two hemispheres had been surgically divided. This means that his left brain does not know what his right brain is thinking, and visa versa. The researcher had a device which could flash visual messages to one side of the brain only. When his right brain was flashed "smile", the boy smiled. When it was flashed "tap", he tapped his fingers on the table. When he was signalled "walk", he got up and walked off. The researcher asked him why he was doing this. This was a verbal inquiry, processed by the boy's left hemisphere. This half of the brain had not had the command and did not know why the boy had got up. However, it provided a perfectly good reason: "Going home to get a Coke".

Human beings are creators of stories, both the ones we tell to ourselves and those we tell to others. By telling stories we make sense of our lives.

Narratives give meaning to our lives. They provide a way to communicate abstract ideas and to gain self-understanding and interpretation of events (Brody, 1991). This is the process by which we construct our own realities about ourselves and the world.

By changing the stories we can change our social realities. Human beings will continue to create myths, beliefs, theories, morals and laws. Knowing that these are created and not absolutes need not destroy our respect for the human species nor what we create. A healthy society creates useful, effective and appropriate stories about itself and its people. It is also flexible enough to adjust those stories or create new ones as conditions change. Beliefs may not be absolute but they can still be very useful and serve us well.

So, the meaning of a piece of behaviour is not inherent in that behaviour. It is assigned to it by social agents, and can vary widely with context and time. Behaviour which is sinister in one context or period may be acceptable or even commendable in another.

This is obvious in the case of wartime and peacetime behaviours. It's not too difficult to tell whether one's country is at war or not, and we adjust accordingly. No problem.

Less obvious are shifts of meanings assigned to sexual behaviour. Despite their high variability from culture to culture and from time to time, they normally carry a form of local absolute value wherever they are found. It is not wise to challenge them openly without the risk of social sanctions.

Sexuality as a social construct

Human beings are identified as male or female from the moment of birth (or even before birth, in an increasing number of cases). Usually the very first comment when a baby is born is "It's a girl!" or "It's a boy!".

And, while maleness and femaleness are readily determined by physical sexual characteristics, masculinity and femininity are highly variable, acquired qualities. We learn to be masculine or feminine in terms laid down by our immediate social environment.

For example, in our culture, when a man whistles at a passing woman it is usually seen as a sexually harassing act. In other cultures (or thirty years ago) the woman might well take it as a compliment. A woman who exposes her breasts in public today is considered sexually provocative, and she may be charged with indecent exposure. However, until this century, in many different parts of the world it was totally acceptable for native women to wear no clothes on their upper bodies. In these cultures, naked breasts were not seen as sexually exciting or immoral.

The early sexologist, Havelock Ellis, told a poignant story (Havelock Ellis, 1936; Weeks 1981). A respectable married woman who leads social purity movements and advocates sexual chastity, discovers by reading a booklet on "solitary vice" that she has been unwittingly practising masturbation for years without realising it. "The profound anguish and hopeless despair of this woman in the face of what she believed to be the moral ruin of her whole life cannot well be described".

The insertion of a finger into the anus of a young boy by an adult man is generally considered to be a perverted and indecent act. This same behaviour may be socially acceptable, however, if the man is a doctor and it is done in the course of a medical examination. The acts may be identical but performed for very different reasons.

So the perceived intent of a behaviour colours our interpretation of it. To this extent our sexuality is sited more in our heads than in our bodies.

There is nothing intrinsically given about sexuality - it is defined by the society and culture of our times.

The politics of sexuality

There have always been groups of people oppressed, stigmatised or excluded from conventional society for adopting different sexual identities. What is considered deviant varies from culture to culture. Typically, homosexuals and prostitutes have often attracted negative attention. In some cultures all women are excluded from public life.

The power held by different groups of people and political policies also helps shape contemporary concepts of sexuality (Foucault, 1976; Weeks, 1987). For example, San Franscisco has been a focus for homosexual men in the last few decades. They are now a significant organised section of the population. They have political and commercial clout and have contributed to a public acceptance of homosexual identity.

Until the second half of the nineteenth century, abnormal sexual behaviour was the concern of the Church and the Courts. As medicine became standardised and professional, it broadened its compass to include sexuality. Abnormal behaviour which was previously seen as illegal or immoral was now seen as sick. Sexual perversions were relabelled as sexual illnesses.

For example, homosexual activity had for centuries been considered a sin and a crime. This century has seen homosexuality identified as a psychiatric illness, which has unfortunately proved resistant to treatment. A more recent trend still has been towards decriminalisation and considering it as a variation of normal, although the gay movement still faces much opposition to this view (Money, 1991).

In some parts of the world, homosexuality has held little or no stigma, and may even assist in achieving a higher social status. Classical Greek culture idealised the boy/man sexual relationship. A study of homosexuality amongst Swahili Moslems of Mombasa (Caplan, 1987) shows that switching to male homosexuality or lesbianism in later life may enable individuals to participate more fully in Mombasa life.

Female sexuality has similarly undergone many changes in the way it's perceived. Judaic tradition saw sensuality as a spiritual blessing. It was accepted that Jewish women enjoyed making love, and indeed Jewish law stated that a husband must have intercourse with his wife at the very minimum once a week (on the Sabbath). His failure to do so gave her grounds for divorce.

Jesus' teachings (which were also traditional Jewish beliefs) were that life should be celebrated and God should be blessed for his gifts of sensual pleasures (Fox, 1981). As it fell under the Greek and Roman traditions of asceticism however, Christianity adopted the very opposite view: that human sexual lust was essentially evil, and carnal urges should be struggled against.

Thus, for Jews, married couples were expected to make love before attending the Synagogue on the Sabbath. The Christian Church, however, forbade its members to receive Communion unless they had been celibate the night before.

Throughout the Middle Ages, the Church's teachings seemed to have little impact on European peasantry, who apparently lived sexually loose and bawdy lives. For many centuries, many writers claim that there was little or no shame or guilt associated with sexual practices. There were very few codes as to what was considered indecent or obscene, and sex was frankly discussed and seldom hidden from family view. Families often ate and slept together in a single room.

With the nineteenth century came a sexual revolution. The Industrial Revolution radically altered the balance of economic and social power in Europe. Those who thrived tended to share a moral ethic which regarded wealth as the proper and obvious reward for living a Christian (ie. Puritan) life.

Sexuality was reserved for procreation rather than enjoyment, to take place only in the privacy of the bedroom. For women it was seen as a duty rather than a pleasure. It was the age of "lie back and think of England". An image emerged of women being "pure", which translated roughly as "having no sexual needs". The ideal woman was conceived of as fragile, weak and emotionally vulnerable. Women who manifestly enjoyed or flaunted their sexuality were stigmatised.

In all this there was a strange inconsistency. Passionless though they might be, middle-class women were yet readily able to arouse sexual desires in men, who needed assistance in controlling their "baser natures". Women were viewed as potentially dangerous exciters of male lust. Tablecloths extended to the floor, and even chairs frequently wore skirts, lest sight of the legs inflame a passing man's fancy.

This ability to sexually allure was exploited by the numerous "fallen women". A double standard was established of private morality but public vice. There may have been domestic virtue in middle class homes, but use of prostitutes was widespread.

The Industrial Revolution was also accompanied by a shift in the perceived source of power. Monarchy traditionally rested its power on its divine right to rule. Social order was maintained by the king, his courts and his army, and then a hierarchy of aristocracy and gentry all the way down to the village squire. The source of authority was always from above.

With the emergence of a wealthy middle class as the effective new power in society, the decision-making process was drawn downwards. The Monarchy became constitutional and more effective power rested with Parliament.

Legislation reflected the needs of the new governing class. Economic regulations protected property. Police, rather than the army, were established to maintain social order. Physical well-being, good health and long life were now considered valuable in the population at large to maintain a productive work force, and public sanitation procedures were introduced and enforced. Industrialisation required a move to urbanised population and a compliant organised labour force.

For the first time, governments became aware of populations as a source of economic and political power. In 1978 Thomas Malthus introduced the argument that population increases faster than its means of support, and advocated moral restraint as a control. There was also a fear that the lower classes were breeding faster than the upper ones and would dilute racial purity.

An individual's sexual practices became a public issue. Child rearing was no longer seen as an individual concern. By controlling sexual activity and restricting procreation to within marriage, the state could direct population size. This heralded the rise of state intervention within the family, a trend which persists today, with the state having ever-increasing powers of influence and decision-making over parents. State control of sexuality was supported by religious sanctions. Most of the world's religions, including Catholicism, Islam and Hinduism, still advocate strict sexual controls.

The closing years of the nineteenth century and the early years of the twentieth saw the puritanical image of women gradually replaced by one which emphasised equality. Women won the right to vote, took a greater role in public life, and saw service under fire in two world wars. By the middle of this century their equality began to extend into sexual matters. Antibiotics removed the dread of sexually transmitted disease, and contraception became simpler and safer. Women began to reown their sexuality, and it became socially acceptable for them to take the initiative in sexual activity, which was seen as a healthy and liberating experience. This is covered in more detail in the next chapter.

However, women's social conditioning continued to emphasis nurturing and caring activities. This is reflected by the way for many women sexuality expresses an emotional bond and not primarily coitus and orgasm.

The last decade has seen a return to anti-sexual beliefs. New diseases such as Herpes and AIDS have replaced the old bogeys of syphilis and gonorrhoea, and, if anything, are even more frightening. Promoting fear of sexual violation and rape is an effective means of denying women their right to sexual self-determination. Women are again presented as powerless victims of men's violent sexual urges.

Victorian society attempted to suppress sexuality, and developed euphemisms to prevent "social evils" being directly discussed. Paradoxically, their very refusal to talk about it made sexuality a major social issue, "*the* secret which put it at the heart of the discourse" (Foucault, 1976; Weeks, 1981). This preoccupation with sexual issues continues today with persistent emphasis on sex by the media and advertising, despite the increasingly repressive attitudes of the 1990s.

Cycles in beliefs and attitudes

A look at human history also reveals the cyclical nature of what is considered "normal" or moral. Fashions change, and what is acceptable to one generation may become taboo to the next. A good example of this is the anti-masturbation movement which lasted from the late eighteenth century until the early twentieth. In 1758 a Swiss physician, Simon Tissot, theorised that semen loss, especially from masturbation (or onanism), caused disease and in particular, syphilis. It was almost universally believed that masturbation caused a variety of physical and mental conditions, including fatigue, consumption, blindness, insanity and dementia.

There followed a massive campaign to prevent children engaging in this dangerous act, which included some very excessive methods of prevention. There were a variety of restraining devices which immobilised the hands or encased the genital region in armour. Acid burns or electro thermal cautery were used to make masturbation too painful. Surgical techniques employed included circumcision, castration, excision of the clitoris, and stitching together of the labia (Howitt, 1992). These methods were of course accompanied by messages evoking terrible guilt and fear should the child persist in his or her evil ways.

Kellogg (of cornflakes fame) and Graham (who developed Graham's crackers) were both advocators of "healthy living" and campaigned extensively to stamp out masturbation. Kellogg developed a list of behaviours which he considered were likely indicators to parents that their child was masturbating. This extensive list included such problems as nightmares, trouble with school work, over-eating, bedwetting, shyness, fearfulness or excessive boldness.

The essence of Victorian society was its contradictory attitude towards sex: women were pure with no interest in sex beyond procreation, yet they were dangerously liable to stir men's passions. Children were considered innocent and asexual on the one hand, yet as easy prey to sexual corruption on the other. They were taught they had to struggle incessantly against their own wicked urges.

Scientific discoveries gradually disproved the belief that semen loss caused syphilis or other illnesses, and these days it is largely accepted that masturbation does an individual no harm. The inherent anti-sexualism, however, has resurfaced in another form.

In many ways it can be seen that the sexual messages of last century are those now proffered by the sexual abuse industry in a different guise, which is the main topic of this book. Behavioural lists virtually identical to Kellogg's are now presented as indicators of sexual abuse. Children are again presented as asexual beings, and excessive masturbation is now considered one of the signs of "childhood sexualisation" and hence an indicator of abuse by an adult.

Another belief currently enjoying a cyclical revival is that of the ideology of witch-craft and satanism of the sixteenth and seventeenth centuries (Money, 1991; Bravos, 1991). In general, society has considered that children are not competent to testify in court, and that hearsay is inadmissible as evidence. However, special rules were used in witch-craft cases, in the belief that "out of the mouths of babes comes truth". Many women were burnt as witches on the uncorroborated evidence of young children. Often these cases depended on children's out-of-court (hearsay) statements. If they did testify, the children were not obliged to face the accused in court and it was not permitted to cross-examine them.

Once accused of witch-craft, there was a presumption of guilt which made it virtually impossible for the accused to prove her innocence. "Confessions" were often extracted after interrogation and torture.

The current allegations of satanic ritual abuse follow an alarmingly similar pattern. Belief in the dogma that "children don't lie about abuse" has lead to special rules of prosecution for child abuse cases. Children are considered competent to testify in sexual abuse cases; their hearsay evidence is often accepted, and they may not have to appear in front of the alleged offender in court. The belief that an allegation of sexual abuse by a child must be true, and that sexual offenders usually deny it, means that there is a presumption of guilt in sexual abuse cases. A falsely-accused father may be denied future access to his child unless he "confesses" and accepts "treatment". If he continues to proclaim his innocence he is likely to get double the sentence.

The stories currently elicited from children when interrogators are investigating allegations of satanic abuse are remarkably similar to those told for hundreds of years. Early Christians, witches in the sixteenth and seventeenth centuries, Gipsies and Jews (even to the Hitler era) have all been accused of ritualistic atrocities, child sacrifice and cannibalism. Despite hundreds of investigations, police in the United States, Britain and Holland have failed to find objective evidence to verify any of the modern-day satanic ritualistic allegations. This phenomenon is explored in greater depth in Chapter 7.

Moral panics and social scapegoats

Societies generally resist changes in their beliefs and values, although these may submerge and resurface in another form, as demonstrated above. When traditional views are challenged, individuals and groups with strongly held moral principles will try to enforce their moral dominance, to maintain social stability. Throughout history, this has given rise to the phenomenon of moral panics (Ben-Yehuda, 1990). In the past, moral panics have produced dramatic results, such as witch hunts, mob attacks, and mass legal actions (Weeks, 1987). Sexuality is often the specific target at times of great social stress. Current moral panics focus on human drug-taking and sexual behaviour.

Many people have an intolerance for uncertainty and ambiguity. They are very uncomfortable with unpredictable or paradoxical situations. People with closed belief systems cannot accept that there can be many simultaneous truths, and that people's beliefs are their subjective reality. Such people need to try and force others to share their own beliefs. They define everything as black or white, good or bad, and events are distorted to fit their belief. It is not just in wartime that the first casualty is truth.

Nor do people like to hear anything that goes against their beliefs or wishes. In earlier times they have literally killed the bearer of bad news. These days, they tend to discredit the source of the facts. The media is manipulated to construct a specific social reality. Moral crusaders will cause the spread of misinformation, which may be either exaggerated or even invented. This is condoned by believing that the end justifies the means. The dangers of a specific deviant behaviour are over-emphasised or made up. The aim in doing this is to stop social change and redefine the moral boundaries.

A society where values and events are confused and ambiguous often gives rise to beliefs of conspiracy (Underwager and Wakefield, 1991). The modern day examples of these are beliefs in widespread co-ordinated "sex-rings" involved in kidnapping children, producing child pornography, and indulging in satanic ritual abuse. This will be further expanded in later chapters.

Current Western society can be seen to be in a state of flux and tension. Political and social situations are changing at an alarming rate. Emerging generations lack a sense of social or financial security. Modern economies and politics operate under conditions of uncertainty and confusion, and the current escalation of sexual and other violence is a reflection of this. Added to this is the worsening effects of over-population, diminishing resources and accumulation of toxic wastes.

In such times, it is not surprising that people search for the security of fundamental and absolute beliefs. They are looking for a civilisation with no uncertainties, where they are not required to make choices. The revolutionary movements of the 1960s advocated social freedoms - women, gay, black and civic rights. However they underestimated the staying power of the cultural myths and institutions. Society is very good at co-opting opponents that start out to destroy it.

The liberal left are now the unlikely bedmates of the radical right. Anti-pornography, anti-male feminists have joined forces with pro-life fundamentalist Christians in a moral crusade against sex-abusing men. The feminists believe that any denial of the apparent epidemic of abuse demonstrates that men still do not admit the way they secretly victimise women and children by rape, wife beatings and incest. The fundamentalists believe in the secret conspiracies of those who do Satan's work, who perform perverted deeds. Both agree on the widespread terrible evil being performed by men, presume that those accused are guilty, and advocate that they should be severely punished or even killed. Recent surveys indicate that well over half the American public support the death penalty for sex crimes.

At times of deep social and political stress, societies look for scapegoats to blame for the conflict (Ben-Yehuda, 1990). The original scapegoat was a live animal sacrificed by the Jewish High Priest in the wilderness to atone for himself and his people. Sadly, this symbol of blame has been replaced by groups of people believed to have caused the unrest. This is often easier than acknowledging the social forces in effect, over which people may have little control. Early Christians, 15th century witches, Gipsies, Jews, blacks and communists in the McCarthy era have all served as social scapegoats. In the current climate, sex offenders are filling this role.

In the world today there are any number of paradigms and stories about stories which claim to be "the answer", the key to the future. Human beings will always generate theories, beliefs and possible solutions to perceived conflicts. The choice is between taking these stories lightly, or adopting the fundamentalist approach of accepting one story as "the truth" and denying or repressing all other stories.

If a country contains many subcultures, it must develop tolerance and understanding that there can be many ways of viewing and interpreting the world. A legal framework is required to ensure the safety of the people. Such regulations need to be kept to a minimum however, to ensure the rights of all to freedom of speech and religious beliefs are not infringed.

If an individual holds a belief that there are no absolutes, his or her behaviour will not be ruled by what is defined as moral or right by other people's beliefs. Instead, he or she is faced with a series of moral choices, where decisions must be made about the meaning and intent of specific acts and their predicted outcomes. Such people are on a never-ending path of understanding and re-understanding life, constructing and reconstructing rules about their relationships with themselves and others.

Such a moral freedom demands a high degree of personal responsibility, and it is not surprising that many people feel threatened or even terrified by such a prospect, especially if the freedom is being exercised by somebody else. It is very understandable that they look without to fundamentalist beliefs for the answers. For some, this leads to the simplistic and unrealistic belief that a return to monogamous family life would solve our social problems, and that any relationships outside of this model reflect an aberration which threatens our stability.

In reality, we have cities teeming with people lacking in occupational, social and spiritual direction, with the loss of the tribe, culture and creed that once provided their identity. With the current diversity of living arrangements and life-styles, new models are urgently needed to help people find the meaning and focus they require to lead creative productive lives.

Issues of personal identity continue to be integrally related to our beliefs about sexuality. These affect the ways we structure families and raise children. Contemporary political forces and state intervention practices will be major influences on the way we construct our personal realities. This book explores the way beliefs about childhood sexual abuse have been constructed, and the effects this is having on our social fabric.

2. Sex in the 20th Century

Women's role in a pre-technological world

Throughout most of human history, a high birth-rate has been necessary for our survival. Before modern technology, death rates from starvation, disease and warfare were high. For tribes and cultures to survive, it was important that their women produced many children. In most cultures, a woman's main function in life was seen as having and raising children.

Various strategies and rules developed in different cultures and races which effectively made women subservient to child care.

Being a wife and mother represented women's total fulfilment. Women depended on men to support them in achieving this end. They often relied on them for protection from external dangers, or for food and shelter. It was the belief of many cultures that women were physically, intellectually and sometimes spiritually inferior to men. In most societies, women were seen as men's property, chattels to be exchanged for goods and services on occasion. Conquering warriors viewed their enemies' women as booty to be raped. Women were one of the spoils of war along with looted property. Women relied on men for their protection, but the price they paid was their freedom and autonomy.

Emancipation of women in the twentieth century

In the last seventy years, industrial, scientific and medical advances have improved material living standards dramatically throughout much of the world. Most people can now expect to live longer, more children survive to become adults, and population levels have climbed to the extent that they now threaten to outstrip the earth's capacity to provide for them. If we are to survive as a species, we must raise smaller families, we must find ways to improve our production of basic food supplies, and we must also find ways to reduce the pollution and waste that results from many industrial processes.

Particularly in the west, many of these goals seem to be achievable. Not only that, more and more people are accepting that they are important goals. Consequently, social change in the west has been dramatic. Women can vote. They have equal rights in education. They have access to and use birth control and abortion. Jobs such as cooking meals and household cleaning take less time. In short, they have become free and competent to take their place in the workforce, and have earned a degree of equality that would have seemed impossible even fifty years ago.

These are positive achievements, and the Women's Liberation Movement of the sixties and seventies has much to be proud of. Present day feminists continue to address remaining inequalities. Most women still do more than half the housework, even if they are working fulltime. Many men still do not accept female equality and resist it vigorously. Our social structure is still a hierarchy run by the same white, male group that has traditionally suppressed women and non-whites.

Sexual reform accelerated in the middle of this century with the development of penicillin and the contraceptive pill. Now there was reliable treatment for syphilis and gonorrhoea, along with effective contraception. As a move towards equality, the Women's Liberation movement encouraged women to experiment with sexual relationships other than monogamous marriage, a freedom previously only condoned for men. It was a natural progression of the battle for women's rights to vote, and for equal educational opportunities and careers. Women's sexual freedom peaked in the 1960s and 1970s. This was a time of affluence and abundance in the west. Economies were booming and jobs easily available. In this climate of wealth and optimism, young people could afford the luxury of challenging social standards.

The anti-sex movement of the 1980s and 1990s

The last decade has seen an economic downturn in the west. For the first time in many developed countries, including Britain, America and Australasia, there is a generation who cannot expect to have better lives than their parents. They have less chance of getting a good education, a job or a home of their own. It seems unlikely that their country's prosperity will get better in their life-times. They face shrinking supplies of food, energy and other resources. These problems are magnified by worsening over-population and environmental damage from technology and toxic wastes.

Our society has moved from a time of hope and freedom (the "love and peace" era of the 60s and 70s) to one of fear. A movement away from sexual freedom emerged at the beginning of the 1980s. Like any form of change, sexual liberation was not seen as desirable by everyone. The staying power of traditional beliefs and institutions was under-estimated by the idealistic revolutionaries of the "free love" era. Sexual reforms faced religious, political, legal and social opposition, which has continued to grow. There are some who blame sexual freedom for causing the rise in social violence, the breakdown of the family and the destruction of the moral fabric of society.

Personal fear often results in a search for a vulnerable scapegoat. Sexual freedom, especially for women, has little in the way of tradition to support it, and much pre-WW2, pre-contraceptive, pre-Women's Liberation tradition was waiting in the wings for an opportunity to re-assert itself with a triumphant "I told you so!". In the early 1980s herpes infection was suddenly exaggerated by the media as a terrible, new, and untreatable disease. Marriages broke up, people were sued and/or ostracised, and a flourishing counselling industry arose to provide support for sufferers. Some believed their lives had been destroyed by catching this incurable sexually transmitted disease. In fact, genital cold sores were not new - they have probably been a fact of life for centuries.

One consequence of all this publicity was that the incidence of herpes actually increased. There was virtually panic at what was seen as a herpes epidemic. Ironically enough, studies have shown that anxiety about herpes makes it more likely that attacks will be more frequent and more serious.

In 1981 the human immunodeficiency virus (HIV) was diagnosed. After treatment for syphilis had become available, for a couple of decades the world had been potentially free of lethal STDs. Now there was another killer venereal disease to deal with, the as yet untreatable AIDS. This disease could have been custom-made to support the views of people opposed to open sexuality. The last deadly outbreak of a venereal disease was the syphilis epidemic of last century. It was accompanied by a massive anti-sexual reaction that at its peak had the legs of chairs and tables covered lest they excite men's lust and inflame their thoughts. A comparable hysteria threatens to accompany the AIDS epidemic.

The reaction against sexual freedom has led to an increase in social controls. For example, in the United States in 1984, new laws were introduced which limit many sexual activities. The age of consent is now eighteen years, not sixteen. Explicit sex education literature is subject to censorship. The definition of sexual abuse has been broadened to include "bad touch". Most areas of sex research have now been banned (Money, 1991). It is against the law in the States to own a picture (a photo, video or painting) that shows naked genitals or female breasts of anyone under eighteen years of age. This means it is now a crime to take naked pictures of your own babies and children. If your baby is a girl, you may not even photograph her topless!

I suggested earlier that we are currently in the midst of a moral panic. At such times, social controls over-ride any moves towards personal freedoms. It is not difficult to find evidence of this. Our society is confronted by ever-increasing changes from all directions. We face political, economic and social upheaval. In multicultural societies, most people no longer have the support of firm religious or social beliefs. These tend to be the characteristics of strongly monocultural societies, or those where one culture is strongly dominant and able to exert sufficient pressure on its minority groups.

Amongst other things, society is beset by worsening physical and sexual violence. Uncertainty and confusion leaves people grasping for ways to obtain social stability. For some, a return to monogamous family life is seen as a way to solve our social problems. Relationships outside of this model are believed to be a threat to society, and therefore not to be tolerated. This has meant a return to fundamental right-wing Christianity for an increasing number of people. Muslim countries are similarly experiencing a move towards fundamentalist Islam. Although the actual religious values might be different, the impulse is the same - a counter to personal freedoms.

Our society could be seen to be founded on colonialism and sexism. From this perspective, white males can be seen to be the cause of our current social evils. For some feminists, men are seen as the continuing oppressors. For some, all men are potential rapists. In this world view, alleged child sex offenders are politically correct and acceptable targets for blame.

Modern feminist analysis

Early women's rights groups fought for equal opportunities with men. Their goals were to give women equal standing alongside men, but not necessarily to replace them. Suffragettes sought freedom to vote, but they did not challenge the traditional family, social and religious values of their times.

Much of modern feminism is involved in describing man's traditional relationships with women as abuse of power. Men are oppressors, to blame for women's subservience. Solutions to remaining problems tend to involve blame, punishment and disempowerment of men rather than empowerment of women which marked the earlier phases of women's liberation. The resulting bitterness and hostility towards men does little to build healthy relationships between men and women.

Return of the double standard

At the height of the sexual revolution, sexual freedom was advocated for both men and women. Society had operated with a double standard and this was recognised and challenged. This standard had condoned promiscuity for men but not women. Young men "sowed their wild oats" but sexually active young women were "sluts". Women should not initiate sex, and they should say "no" even when they meant "yes". Sex was viewed as something men wanted, and women resisted.

Liberalisation of sexual attitudes led to the scientific study of sexuality (Kinsey et al 1953; Masters and Johnson, 1970). It was confirmed that women had strong sexual drives, and the female orgasm was acknowledged and studied. Medical developments led to reduced risks of catching sexually transmitted diseases or having unwanted pregnancies. For the first time, many women were free to discover and enjoy their sexuality as active participants and initiators.

The last decade has seen a return of the double standard. The media and advertising constantly display what is considered to be the desirable image for a woman. She should appear sexually attractive to men. Make-up, sexually-alluring clothes and many other consumer products are marketed with this in mind. A woman receives powerful messages that she should pay close attention to how she looks, her body shape and appearance. This objectifies her, and damages her integral sense of self-worth.

Moreover, while her goal is to be sexually attractive to men, all men, there is a clear counter statement that it is not acceptable to be sexually active outside of monogamous marriage. Presented with this conflicting message of sexual allurement and rebuff, it is not surprising that many men are confused as to what constitutes consent. From a woman's point of view, she may feel coerced into a sexual experience, or even raped. However, from the man's perspective, her resistance might be interpreted as modesty, and that she is really "asking for it".

It can be seen how a girl progressively learns her role as victim, just as a boy learns his as oppressor.

The ideology of victimology

Many of the gains won for women's sexual freedom in the 1960s and 1970s still remain. Society is much more tolerant of single mothers, and de facto relationships are commonplace. However, the current rise in prevalence of anti-sexual attitudes is promoted by the unlikely association of fundamental Christianity and radical feminism. Orthodox churches decry all sex except for procreation within marriage. Radical feminism believes that the power differential between men and women prevents an equal relationship and makes all heterosexual relationships potentially abusive of women. Relationships where the man is older than the woman or in a position of relative authority (for example, better educated or in a higher position with respect to his work) are seen as exploitive. Both views unite in working to severely limit sexual relationships between men and women.

The women's rights movement encouraged many women to be individuals first and wives and mothers second. They discovered ways to claim their own personal power instead of merely filling socially prescribed and limited roles. They were able to explore and develop their own potential, and follow educational paths and careers of their own choosing. Many women have been successful in this regard.

Modern-day feminism tends to focus on the perceived imbalances continuing between men and women. To this end it is useful to view men as potential oppressors, and women as victims of their oppression. Redress is sought by disempowering men.

It is believed that women should be protected from men and positively discriminated for. They should be assisted in gaining places in educational institutions and higher status, more powerful positions in their employment.

Paradoxically, such policies maintain women as dependent victims, unable to achieve these ends on their own merits. It covertly assumes that women are still incapable of relationships with men on an equal footing. Ironically, such a belief system sacrifices women's power by redefining them as victims requiring protection and assistance.

In some ways it is possible to see the women's movement as having declined from a strong and effective force of eccentric individualists, to groups of self-defined victims obsessed with codes of political correctness and focused on blame (Paglia, 1990).

Unfortunately, such a model does not address issues of how to improve relationships between men and women. Other options to consider could include strong, personally powerful women developing and maintaining relationships with men based on mutual co-operation and respect, rather than competition and power. Emphasis could be on inter-dependence, rather than the dichotomy of independence versus dependency. I suggest that society need not demand that its women be sexually alluring but untouchable. Both boys and girls could be educated that personal achievements are of far more value than looks. Women need not sacrifice personal and family goals for professional success. In such a world, men and women could relate as complementary allies, in trusting, loving and supporting relationships.

3. Growth of the Sexual Abuse Industry

The history of child sexual abuse

Society has not always been as concerned about childhood sexual behaviour as it is at present. In early Greek and Roman times homosexual relationships with young boys were socially acceptable. There were brothels of boy prostitutes, and boys were sometimes castrated as babies to increase their attractiveness as prostitutes later in life (Underwager, 1990).

In medieval Europe, parents would masturbate their children to settle them. Families mostly lived in one room, and children would see adults making love. It was common for adults to touch children's genitals, make sexual gestures to them, and crack crude jokes in their presence (Schultz, 1982). Children would often be married at puberty, or even before.

Attitudes changed around the 18th century. It was no longer acceptable in polite society for children to witness or take part in sexual activity. Children slept separately from adults, and boys played separately from girls. It was no longer acceptable for children to be naked.

Masturbation was considered dangerous, to be watched for and quickly punished. It was believed to have all sorts of terrible effects, including causing mental disorders, weakness, and many physical illnesses. From 1850 to 1900 surgery, including removing the clitoris, cutting nerves to the genitals, cautery to the clitoris and penis, and even castration of boys, was sometimes used to "treat" masturbation. Between 1875 and 1925 there was also the use of constraints such as splints, chastity belts, and tying a child's hands to the bed, to prevent sexual touching. Known as onanism, masturbation was seen by the Victorian bourgeoisie to be a terrible affliction and of epic proportions.

Until the end of the 19th century, there were no laws regarding child abuse. In 1875 the Society for the Prevention of Cruelty to Children (SPCC) was founded in New York. From the 1870s, laws were introduced in the United States protecting children from physical and sexual abuse from adults. However, until the 1950s, child abuse was not seen as a significant social problem.

In the early 1960s Dr Henry Kempe reported results of a survey indicating what he coined the "battered child syndrome". There was suddenly professional and media attention to abused children. Public awareness grew that this was a major problem. New laws were passed to protect children, and the issues moved from private family ones to matters of public policy. Initially, attention was on physically battered children.

Development of the sexual abuse field in the last two decades

Before the 1970s, little was known about sexual abuse. There was no public knowledge, and very little was being seen by public child welfare agencies. When it was reported, disclosures were usually made spontaneously by girls, not elicited by sexual abuse investigators. These girls often believed that what was happening to them was normal in childhood. Alternatively they believed that their horrible experiences had never happened to anyone else, and there was something the matter with them that made it happen.

Often their stories about abuse would be denied by their mothers and others, or they would be blamed for letting it happen. They would usually feel guilty and ashamed. Often child victims of incest would be made to "promise not to tell" by their fathers, and events would be veiled in secrecy. Telling about the abuse would often lead to further unpleasantness with the police, courts and welfare systems. Girls might be blamed by their mothers and siblings for causing the breakup of their family and putting their father in prison. Often, the courts might decide the girl was lying and the offender would get off.

In such situations, it was very unlikely that a girl would make a false complaint of sexual abuse. Health and social workers, especially those with feminist ideologies, recognised that families and society tended to deny that sexual abuse had occurred, or blame a girl for seducing her father. In reaction, they declared that a child's claim of abuse should always be believed. The dictum that "children never lie about abuse" is one of the fundamental beliefs underpinning the sexual abuse field.

Reports of child sexual abuse increased rapidly. Public awareness began to grow, and by the mid 1970s child sexual abuse was identified as the "last frontier" of child abuse awareness (Summit) - an unfortunate expression which was to be reflected only too often in the methods used to deal with the problem.

It was a frontier shared by police and justice department officials, doctors, social workers, psychologists, counsellors and therapists and educators, very few with any experience or training. Specific agencies were set up, and child protection teams formed between disciplines. The major belief systems were laid down swiftly, and reflected the strong feminist influence that had drawn attention to the problem in the first place.

Public concern continued to grow and was fuelled by the extensive media coverage of the subject, still largely defined in its original feminist terms. New Zealand, like other western countries, began to respond to this new public health problem, and in the last 10 years a large and growing industry has appeared to address problems related to child sexual abuse.

Faulty assumptions underpinning the field

In the 4th century BC, Aristotle stated "the least initial deviation from the truth is multiplied later a thousand-fold". Small mistakes at the beginning lead to ever-worsening consequences if these faulty assumptions are not recognised and corrected. Regrettably, many of the beliefs associated with the sexual abuse industry are very shaky indeed, and this has meant that some serious mistakes have been made, despite the integrity and good intentions of those working in the field.

Unfortunately, the developing sexual abuse field has not been open to challenge about these basic assumptions. In this respect, the frontier description is once more an apt one. The sheriff is the guy on the white horse with the star. Anyone who challenges him is by definition on the other side.

Within the mainstream sexual abuse field it is believed that:
- **children do not lie about sexual abuse** (Finkelhor, 1979; Moore, 1985; Saphira, 1987; Crewdson, 1988)
- **1 in 4 girls will be sexually abused before their 16th birthdays, most of them by their father or a close relative or friend** (Finkelhor, 1979; Rush, 1980; Russell, 1984; Saphira, 1985; Mental Health Foundation of New Zealand, 1988; Otago Women's Health Survey, 1990)
- **when sexual abuse is suspected, it almost certainly exists** (McFarlane, 1986; Bass and Davis, 1988)
- **all sexual activity between adults and children is inevitably harmful** (Summit, 1983; Bass and Davis, 1988)
- **sexual abusers will deny their behaviours** (Finkelhor, 1979; Saphira, 1987; Bass and Davis, 1988; Sanford, 1990)

The claim that children never lie about abuse takes no account of the processes by which memory may be distorted and reconstructed. Expectations of interviewers and interrogation techniques can unwittingly influence a child's testimony. This topic will be covered in depth in the following chapter.

Child sexual abuse is a highly emotional area. It involves children, and it involves sex. As yet few workers are prepared to acknowledge that their findings might be coloured by expectation, or by personal belief and value systems, and indeed, any such challenge is vigorously defended.

Health professionals who make such a challenge are seen to be denying that abuse might have happened and are likely to be accused of colluding with abuse. They are especially vulnerable if they are men, who are the usual offenders in sexual abuse. They face the threat of deregistration and other persecution and usually respond by "keeping their heads down" (personal communications).

Sexual abuse workers are also unlikely to recognise when they are motivated by ethical and political goals which may in fact not be in the best interest of the individual children and adults with whom they are working.

I mentioned before that the major belief systems were laid down swiftly. The rapid rise in reported abuse cases required an equally rapid "training" of social workers and other health professionals to deal with the problem, and this was carried out through frequent seminars and workshops, and a quickly assembled "literature" on the subject. Information to the public was disseminated via the media. Much of this information has not undergone vigorous scientific assessment. However, the informal communication network has resulted in the widespread acceptance of these beliefs as facts.

Any belief system which has it as highly likely that challenges to it come from criminals or those who support criminals had better have its beliefs soundly based. Yet the literature of sexual abuse abounds with incidents of opinion claimed as fact without any scientific validation. For example, we have seen the development of diagnostic aids such as anatomically correct dolls; claims made that testifying in front of the defendant will harm a child; the use of untested prevention programmes in schools. All these have become standard procedures without any credible, reliable evidence to support their use (Rogers, 1990; Wakefield and Underwager, 1989).

Lack of professional and ethical scrutiny

Practitioners in the sexual abuse industry are accorded respectability by the professional community without the ethics or science of their practices being professionally scrutinised. They often work in this field with very little academic qualifications or training. Some workers identify themselves as victims of past sexual abuset, and this may be considered by some agencies to be a positive attribute in a therapist. This raises the disturbing possibility that people who have been diagnosed as permanently psychologically damaged are working as sexual abuse counsellors.

I have mentioned the considerable feminist influence in the early training. Feminism, especially radical feminism, tends to distrust traditional methods of professional training and supervision on the grounds that they have been developed by men in a patriarchal system and are therefore tainted (Archer, Wojt and Woodman, 1986; Lee 1986). These values have tended to enter sexual abuse counselling along with matters more properly suited to the training of professional social workers. Where such values are promoted, an insistence on scientific truth is tantamount to labelling yourself as a supporter of the corrupt, male-dominated world of rationalism.

The nature of the network is such that the same beliefs and perspectives continue to be presented. There is in fact a growing body of research findings and writings which address some of these issues differently. However these tend to be published in psychological or sociological scientific journals or books which are not distributed by the network. Some of this material is considered "backlash" literature and is ignored by the industry. It does, however, have a sufficient grounding in rigorous research to demand answers to some of the questions it raises.

An example of the intellectual fudging I have been talking about is at the very foundation of the whole belief system. Many sexual abuse workers claim that "all sensitive well-meaning professionals" would be in agreement as to what constitutes abuse. There will be near-agreement in cases where adults have coercive and non-consenting sexual intercourse with children. However, most cases are neither that extreme nor clear cut. There is in fact a huge variation in how abuse is defined by different agencies and in different locations. Even the age at which a child becomes an adult (the age of consent) varies from 13 to 18 years in the Western world.

Consequently, it is extremely difficult to compare studies and research findings. Many centres have extended their definition to include "bad touch", which tends to inflate their figures of incidence. Some studies do not even clarify what they consider to be sexual abuse. Others use retrospective definitions - their figures include everyone who believes themselves to have been abused as a child, and what actually happened does not need to be specified. I will discuss the problems about definition further in Chapter 5.

The broadening of the definition and over-zealous investigation has lead to extremely high reported prevalence rates. This results in the unfortunate consequence of the existing services becoming overloaded and our limited resources badly taxed. This jeopardises the effective diagnosis of genuine serious child abuse cases.

Sexual abuse workers usually operate under the assumption that all sexual activity between adults and children is inevitably harmful. This is not actually supported by the limited sociological and psychological evidence currently available. However, when this is assumed, investigators use emotive language which gives a serious bias to the proceedings. For example, workers may describe all sexual experience between children and adults as abuse, victimisation, exploitation, assault or molestation. Professionals who use such labels unwittingly make value judgements disguised as diagnoses (Nelson, 1989). It has been suggested that the neutral word participant be used instead of perpetrator (or offender) and victim until the type of involvement has been established. Similarly, the term intergenerational sex could be used until the facts of the case are known. This expression includes incest and minor/adult sexual contact which does not involve relatives, and both abusive and non-abusive childhood sexual experiences.

Victimology and the sexual abuse industry

Current management of sexual abuse relies on the broader principles of victimology, which is a philosophy with increasing influence in the Western world. I will cover this topic in greater depth later. Basically, this is a viewpoint that sees victims needing treatment, and perpetrators deserving punishment. The agent of victimisation (the perpetrator) should be segregated from society, disciplined or even eliminated (Money, 1991). A get-tough stance is endorsed towards child sexual offenders. Some offender treatment programmes (for example Dreibratt, 1982) advocate an authority-based approach where offenders undergoing treatment should be confronted, challenged, and approached with scepticism and cynicism by the therapist. Practitioners offering treatment for sexual abusers are taught that they must not offer their clients trust, acceptance or caring (MacLeod and Saraga, 1988). It is largely believed that sexual offenders are intractable, and will continue to reoffend. The emphasis in treatment is therefore on punishing sexual illness rather than restoring sexual health.

The conflict between the evidence-gathering and treatment roles of workers

This view of the world places workers investigating abuse in a position of unreconcilable conflict between forensic evidence-gathering and therapy. Discipline as a method of treatment belongs to the adversarial tradition of the law, not the humanity of medicine. It is not possible to serve Hippocrates, the Healer, at the same time as Hammurabi, the Law-giver. Human sexuality workers unintentionally become defacto "undercover agents of the social service and health-care secret police" (Money, 1991). Investigators work under codes of confidentiality but are required to report confidential information to the criminal justice system. They run programmes of disciplinary retraining euphemistically called therapy. In many places mandatory reporting has been introduced whenever the possibility of sexual abuse is suggested. In these cases, the mandatory reporting directive over-rides the confidentiality of a consultation.

In the last decade, then, New Zealand has developed a sexual abuse industry in parallel with other western countries, especially the USA. At the foundation of their work lies some unacknowledged wrong assumptions. This is leading to ever-worsening consequences, particularly in regard to false allegations of abuse.

The following chapters explore some of these issues further. It will be seen where blindly following these basic premises is taking us, and some suggestions are offered for alternative ways to view the situation and manage the very real problems of sexual abuse.

4. Can Memories always be Believed and Trusted?

"Man's most valuable trait is a judicious sense of what not to believe"
Euripides, 412 BC.

One of the difficulties a defendant will face in defending himself against a charge of child sexual abuse is the assumption by investigating social workers that children never lie about abuse.

It is claimed that children and adolescents seldom or never make false allegations about sexual abuse - the child must always be believed (Sgroi, 1982; Yates and Musty, 1988). The argument is that "a child couldn't possibly know about abuse unless it happened" (Kiefer, 1989). It is believed that children have no motives for false claims. The very fact that they have told proves their contact with harmful sex. I have explained how this belief came into being in response to the common reaction of blame and denial these girls used to meet.

By dogmatically sticking to these claims, despite increasing evidence that false allegations do occur, sexual abuse workers risk interfering, and interfering traumatically, in families where nothing harmful has happened. In the past, cases of sexual abuse were rarely discovered unless a child spontaneously told someone about it. These days, more and more cases are alleged only after an adult starts questioning a child. The process this family then faces in its contact with the social welfare and legal services can be very damaging to all concerned. These families face loss of privacy, expensive court battles, and enormous stress and trauma.

Furthermore, large numbers of false claims will reduce the system's ability to give adequate help to those in genuine need (Klajner-Diamond et al, 1987; Everson and Boat, 1989). It is important that children who are being harmed are identified and assisted; it is just as important that other children and their families are not inadvertently hurt by this process.

In most cases of alleged sexual assault, both child abuse and adult rape, there is no other witness to what actually happened. Occasionally, there might be found semen, sexually transmitted infection, or injuries consistent with the alleged assault. Usually, however, the evidence relies on the uncorroborated statements of both parties. The legal system, which is very "black and white" and adversarial in nature, simplifies this to "one person is lying and the other telling the truth".

Where it is claimed that victims never lie, there is a presumption that the accused is always guilty.

Furthermore, what is not taken into account are the ways memories may be genuinely inaccurate. Lying implies deliberate and wilful malice. A child may not be lying, but what she or he says may not be factually correct (Zeitlin, 1987). There are many processes and influences by which a child can come to report information about events which never actually happened (Warren-Leubecker, 1991) and these will be explored further in this chapter.

Issues of suggestibility and the accuracy of memory

The rapid growth of the sexual abuse field meant that a fairly small group of people were responsible for training and educating the others. Networks quickly developed, and those writing about sexual abuse based their work on the theories of those initial workers. Most of the huge body of literature now available has this same base.

The relatively uniform thinking this has produced in the industry today means that any books that are published which offer challenge to its beliefs are generally dismissed as part of a "backlash".

In the past two to three decades there has been considerable research in the field of memory.

Much of the scientific debate about memory appears in the more academic psychological and sociological journals not read by social workers, counsellors and therapists. I was unaware of it myself until my own misgivings prompted me to look further than the assumptions I had been given to work with.

Current theories and research findings about the nature of memory clearly demonstrate that our memories are reconstructions, not photographic records. Our memories will often be very different from what actually happened. Eye witnesses to traffic accidents are notorious for telling divergent stories. And in one celebrated incident in New Zealand during the Vietnam war protests, the defendants were found guilty by a magistrate despite four police witnesses telling mutually contradictory stories from the witness box. The magistrate commented that if they all had the same story, he would have suspected collusion.

When we are faced with two people reporting very different memories about an event in the past, it is quite possible that neither is lying yet neither is accurate about what actually happened.

Influences that distort memory
Memories of childhood events are frequently inaccurate. What causes them to become inaccurate has been well-researched and is well-documented. When memory reconstructions are subjected to these contaminating influences, the stories recalled can become exaggerated, distorted and even totally fabricated.

Sexual abuse workers acknowledge the unreliability of human memory. They deal with the situation very simply. They make their own field an exception. Children, they say, do not lie about core events, and sexual abuse is a core event.

Even this exception has its exceptions....

Children do not lie about sexual abuse unless they are denying it. Interviewers characteristically ignore or challenge children's denials that abuse occurred.

The notion of a core event has not so far been supported or even suggested by any substantive research. It is simply an unsupported assertion by the sexual abuse workers which pre-empts challenge.

Distortion by time
As time goes by, children's tendency to make recall errors will increase. A time delay between a child's observation or experience and his or her testimony reduces the accuracy of the testimony (Lipton, 1977). They will tend to modify their stories with additional information or distortions (Saywitz, 1987). The same is also true for adults - memories fade as time passes.

Distortion as the result of post-event misinformation
People can produce sincere but inaccurate recollections by unwittingly assimilating misleading information from others.

Many studies have been made on the effects of misinformation (Loftus, 1975; Loftus, Burns and Miller, 1978; Cole and Loftus, 1979; Loftus and Davies, 1984; Ceci et al, 1988; Loftus, Korf and Schooler, 1989; Wells, 1980; Lindsay, 1990).

Questions asked after an event can substantially alter a subject's memory of what actually happened. After witnessing a short film, subjects are asked questions which contain implied information. For example, they might be asked where a man went after he picked up a hammer. Assumptions that something was picked up, that the something was a hammer, that it was a man who picked it up, and that he went somewhere with it, may or may not be accurate, but can be successfully implanted in the witnesses' memory as the result of such questioning.

Witnesses have misrecalled stop signs as give-way signs, cars as being blue rather than green, hammers as being spanners, have remembered broken glass or tape-recorders that never existed, and even become convinced they remember large objects such as barns where there were none.

Moreover, subjects of these experiments adamantly defended their suggested memories. Once a memory has been distorted in this way, it is very difficult to retrieve the original memory.

Other studies have shown that misleading information is much more likely to be incorporated into memory if it is provided by someone in authority or trusted by the subject (Dodd and Bradshaw, 1980). This is relevant when alleged sexual abuse victims are asked leading questions by parents, social workers, police or counsellors.

Extreme confidence in knowing a memory is right does not in fact correlate with accuracy. Studies have shown that people are often wrong when they are certain they know the right answer, and their confidence for suggested memories can be as great as that reported for memories based on actual perceptions (Fischhoff et al, 1977; Schooler et al, 1986). One study showed that even when subjects were warned in advance that they were likely to be given some misinformation about what had happened, they still incorporated the suggestions into their recall and confidently insisted on the accuracy of their memories.

It is very difficult to believe that what one remembers is not true. Almost all conscious memory is based on what we remember, and much of that will in fact be true. This includes memory programmes of everyday tasks such as driving a car. To ask people to question their own memories is in a sense asking them to question their own interpretations of reality, and this may well be threatening to their sense of identity (Dawes, 1992). People will understandably believe in their own memories.

Both adults and children are susceptible to memory distortion by suggestion, especially when a considerable period of time has elapsed between the initial event and the introduction of the misinformation.

There is now substantial documentation of how post-event information can change a person's report of his or her memory of what happened. What has not been established yet, is whether this alters the original memory permanently, or whether the old memory still exists but is made inaccessible by the new one. This is currently being debated vigorously by researchers in the field (Loftus and Schooler, 1985; McCloskey and Zaragoza, 1985; Zaroga 1991; Lindberg 1991).

Distortions as a result of interviewer expectations

When children are asked questions, even when these are intended to be unanswerable, they will almost invariably give answers. Children are practised at making sense of situations, and will attempt to answer even the most bizarre questions. In a study by Hughes and Grieve, 1983, children were asked questions like "Is red heavier than yellow?" and "Is milk bigger than water?". Children under seven years of age almost never said they did not know or that the question did not make sense; instead, they came up with ingenious responses, such as "red is heavier because it's got more colour" or "milk is bigger because it comes out of bottles". Children expect adults to ask logical questions which must have an answer, and they respond accordingly.

Many studies have demonstrated that the expectations of a questioner colours what is asked and how it is asked. Leading gestures and questions, especially from someone in authority, can cause very significant contamination of memory recall (Vandierendonck and Damme, 1988; Gardner, 1992).

In one study by Clarke-Stewart et al (reported in Ceci and Bruck, 1992), children watched a janitor either cleaning a doll or handling it roughly and suggestively. They were later questioned by interviewers about what they had seen. These interviewers were either neutral, inferred that the janitor had been playing with the doll suggestively, or implied he was only cleaning the doll. The child was then reinterviewed by another interviewer who either reinforced or contradicted the first.

When the interviewer was either neutral or asked questions consistent with what a child had witnessed, children's accounts were factually accurate. However, when the first interviewer contradicted what had happened, children quickly conformed their stories, and ninety per cent answered in agreement with the examiner, rather than relating what had actually happened. When questioned by their parents immediately after the interview and a week later, the children's stories still reflected the interviewer's interpretation of events rather than the real event.

When the second interviewer contradicted the first, the majority of the children changed their stories to now fit with the second examiner.

Distortion as a result of thinking, writing about and discussing a memory

Memories are distorted by the on-going processes of thinking about, writing about and discussing what happened. Mental impressions "firm-up" to give a more and more detailed picture of what is believed to have happened. Repetition of a story often leads to uncertain details later reported as definitely true.

Repeated exposure to stories about similar events leads to a more generalised, non-specific recall (Schwartz, 1982; Slackman and Nelson, 1984; Flinn, 1991). As memories fade, children reconstruct their old scripts by incorporating their remembered information with their growing general knowledge of similar events (Myles-Worsley et al, 1986).

Distortion as a result of sharing memories with other participants

Research indicates that childhood memories are largely learnt by a child's conversation with others (Lindesmith et al, 1986). Pre-verbal memories are often produced by the child's later conversations with parents and others about early events. Personal memories are greatly rooted in the collective memory of groups. Early childhood experiences are commonly filtered through the memories of parents and relatives, who recall incidents from our early lives and hence help us shape our memories (Victor, 1991).

Research shows that group discussion can bias eyewitness testimony, and individuals are liable to change their reported memories of an incident to agree with the group leaders' recall following group discussion of what happened (Hollin and Clifford, 1983). Group discussions about an event will tend to reach a consensus about what happened. Hollin and Clifford's studies showed that group processes produced highly inaccurate -but agreed upon- testimony. This study demonstrated beyond doubt that discussion affects individual testimony.

Distortion from confusion of dream or fantasy with memories of real events

Very young children have difficulty separating reality from fantasy, as anyone who has told monster stories to little ones will know. They often embellish or distort events. For example, bathing may be interpreted as masturbatory, if the child is given the right cues. Children often have difficulty distinguishing memory, fantasy, and memory of fantasy (Rosenfeld et al, 1979). They have a developing imagination and commonly have a tendency to tell extravagant and fantastic falsehoods centred about themselves (Money, 1991).

Adults as well as children can sometimes become confused between performed and imagined actions (Foley and Johnson, 1985). A common example of this is mistakenly thinking you have done something you only intended to do, such as lock the door. The doctrine that children never lie about sexuality flagrantly ignores this knowledge.

It seems that childhood sexual fantasies are very deep-seated. Sigmund Freud tapped into these in his early psychoanalysis work. His initial interpretation of his case-histories was that all his patients had in fact experienced sexual contact with their parents in early childhood. He later came to believe that these virtually universal stories were psychological fiction and developed his theories of oedipal fantasy.

Traditional psychoanalysis now subscribes to the view that the recall is fantasy, although still very important to work through to gain mental health. There is however another school of thought, especially in feminist circles, which believes that Freud's original thinking was correct: that these memories did in fact relate to accurate historical events and that all Freud's patients were in fact victims of incest.

I have examined transcripts of several cases where it is clear that the children involved cannot distinguish between fact and fantasy. In one of these, a six year old boy undergoes thirty-two disclosure interviews with a therapist, all but the very first one involving anatomical dolls. Although he persistently denies that "daddy does naughty things" for most of the interviews, he eventually begins to agree that daddy has molested him. His claims then get more and more extreme and bizarre, eventually involving a wide range of people and animals. Although it is evident that most of these outrageous events could never really have happened, his therapist never challenges him about them. She remains confident he must be telling the truth, even though the stories were clearly in the realm of fantasy.

Distortion as a Result of Current Beliefs and Feelings

Through a process of subjective interpretation of our pasts, we may come to believe in something that never happened. How we reconstruct our memories to fit the present stories of our lives is largely determined by our current beliefs and feelings. This has been established repeatedly in psychological research (Goodmann and Hahn, 1987; Dawes 1989; Loftus, Korf and Schooler, 1989; Loftus and Ketchman, 1991).

It is possible to reframe an experience we found harmless or enjoyed as a child into one that was unpleasant if we now believe that it should not have happened. Similarly, it is possible to reframe a bad experience into a positive one, by focusing on the ways we may have gained from that experience. Indeed, psychotherapy can be viewed as a process of retelling our life stories in a positive and useful way.

Effects of Interviewing Techniques on Memory

When it is appreciated how easily misinformation can change a person's recollection of a past event, it can be seen that extreme care is needed not to contaminate a story when evidence is sought for court proceedings. Children are especially malleable, and what they say has to be carefully considered in the light of the degree and types of influences which have been exerted on them (Wong, 1987).

Children are very eager to please, and will usually tell adults what they think they want to hear. Very young children may learn expected responses, even from conversations not addressed to them (Oshima-Takane, 1987). Part of human nature is to try and excuse oneself from responsibility and to please others by saying what they want to hear (Pride, 1986). Even small babies will crawl away from a mess they know they should not have made and try to look like someone else has done it.

In an interview situation, it is very easy for the truth to be distorted. A child may understand more and more what the questioner wants to hear, learn the story by repetition, and come to experience the subjective reality that abuse has happened when it has not. Children can easily be trained to believe something occurred through systematic manipulation. There are a large number of studies which demonstrate this (Underwager, 1986; Wakefield and Underwager, 1988; Underwager R and Wakefield H, 1990; Coleman and Clancy, 1990; Ornstein 1991).

Studies by Underwager and Wakefield have been made of hundreds of cases of sexual abuse allegations. They examined tapes of interviews (audio and video), statements, transcripts and psychological reports, and found a common pattern in the way children are interrogated, both in America and other western countries. I have similarly looked at transcripts of a number of New Zealand interviews.

Generally, the first thing that starts the process is that an adult notices something about a child such as a behaviour change which he or she believes indicates abuse. This might be any number of signs or actions, such as bed-wetting, a rash on the genitals, being unusually aggressive or getting easily upset, or having bad dreams. The adult questions the child then calls an authority, usually a child protection worker or the police.

Because of the intense feelings aroused by suspicion of sexual abuse, the adult will usually have asked the child suggestive questions, often repetitively. His or her interpretation of the child's responses, along with the initial suspicions, will be passed onto the investigator. If this official believes false allegations seldom occur and that the symptoms described are predictive of abuse, he or she will approach the child with the assumption that abuse has certainly happened. This bias affects the way the child is interviewed and the resulting outcome.

It can be seen from many videotapes of interactions between therapists and children that over-zealous interviewers often use leading questions, cueing of desired responses, praise for desired answers, and manipulated fantasy play which implants ideas about sexual activity. This is a process called "priming" (Herr, 1986; James 1986) and is usually neither deliberate or conscious on the part of the therapist.

When over-enthusiastic interviewers "prime" children in this way, reconstituted memories are gradually implanted, and then shaped by further conversations. The more a child talks about the story with parents and others, the more these pseudomemories become subjectively real (Victor, 1991). As discussed above, once a memory has been distorted, this distortion is very likely to remain (Loftus et al, 1989).

Everyone is suggestible to some degree or another. The authority of the interviewer, as well as the questions asked, can influence the responses of both children and adults (Vandierendonck and Damme, 1988).

Extreme care should be taken to try and get an accurate story from a child while avoiding the effects of misleading suggestions (Fundudis, 1989). Children may not offer much information spontaneously, and whilst prompting may help their recall, it is likely to lead to inaccuracies, especially if a child feels under pressure to give an answer (Kobasigawa 1974, Dent 1982, Dent 1991, Furman and Walden, 1990).

Parents and interviewers should appreciate the influence they may have on a child's story, and realise that the interview itself may greatly distort a child's memories (Ornstein, 1991).

A study of interrogation techniques (Underwager et al, 1986) showed that 60% of the interviewing behaviours of trained examiners involved potentially leading questions, closed questions (require yes or no answers), modelling, and the use of aids. These aids include such tools as anatomically correct dolls, drawings and photos. The evidence produced by these is open to interpretation and they have yet to be substantiated as valid tools for diagnosis (Wong, 1987).

If someone interrogating children believes the allegations are true, whatever a child says will tend to confirm his or her belief. When children deny that anything happened, the interviewer assumes they are too scared to tell. Children are encouraged to be brave and tell, and reassured that what happened was not their fault and they will not be punished.

This can be extremely confusing and distressing for children trapped - and trapped they effectively are - in an interview with a social worker, and separated from their families for weeks and months in welfare care. Finally they will sort out what is happening and give the right responses. I have the record of one interview where an eight year old girl admits that Daddy molested her, after weeks of denials during a series of interrogations. The admission is followed immediately by the request "Will I be able to go home now that I've told?". At that time, she had been in foster care for over two months. When she is still not allowed to go home, she resumes her denials that Daddy has abused her.

Transcripts of many interviews conducted in the United States, Britain and Australasia have demonstrated how bribes and threats are often used (perhaps unwittingly) to get the right responses from children. I have personally examined transcripts from a number of New Zealand cases.

One of these cases involves a four and a half year old girl, Fay (all names changed to maintain confidentiality), whose mother believes the father has sexually abused her during access visits. To date Fay has never admitted it. She has already had nine "disclosure" interviews. This one is the last and is being videotaped and watched by a senior psychologist through a one-way screen.

The session lasts over two and a half hours. Sally, the psychotherapist conducting the interview, repeatedly encourages Fay to undress anatomical dolls and show her what happened. She keeps asking questions about "naughty touching" and ignores Fay when she gives the wrong answer or wants to talk about something else.

Several times Fay tries to tell Sally that she has hidden from her daddy and peeked around the door to watch him urinate. Three or four times she takes the "Daddy doll" to the toilet. Philip, her father, had caught her doing this and told her off. He had also told Sally about this before the sessions started. This incident was clearly a naughty one to Fay, and she returns to it again and again when asked about naughty things that happened at Daddy's. Sally ignores her answers and continues to ask about sexual activities in the bedroom.

Throughout the interview, Sally promises Fay that they will soon be finished. "this is the last, last, last thing", "show me that last, last bit and then we'll go and have a drink and a biscuit and see Mummy", "Truly, we can go and see Mummy very soon". After a hour and a half and nine promises that it's nearly over, Fay is obviously frustrated and exhausted. She lies on the floor while the questions continue. It is more than one hour after this that the session finally ends.

She is constantly asked leading questions, or given two alternatives to chose from. Although Fay has already denied that Daddy does naughty things, she is asked "does he do some of the naughty things with his mouth?" and "shall we look at the naughty things that happened in the bath first or the naughty things that happened in bed?" When presented with two choices, Fay usually answers with the second one.

At one point, Fay says her daddy has kissed her.

S: What sort of kisses were they? Were they dry kisses or wet kisses?
F: Wet. ....
S: Right, was Fay lying down, was she lying on the bed?
F: I don't know.
S: Was she under the bedclothes or on top of the bedclothes?
F: On top.
S: On top of the bedclothes lying on the bed. So let's put Fay there right and she's lying there, has she got her knickers off or her knickers on?
F: Knickers on.

When Fay gives a response that Sally is looking for, she is showered with praise: "What a good good girl!", "You do very well, very very well, what a big help you've been!". Mostly these responses are placing the dolls in suggestive positions after Sally models the "required" actions, such as putting the male doll's mouth on the female doll's vagina.

At the end of the session, Sally concludes that Philip has sexually abused Fay on an ongoing basis, including vaginal touching and oral sex. Although Fay continues to deny it, this is explained by the abuse being so traumatic that she cannot admit it. Sally believes that Fay has given her covert messages of what happened during the interview.

Her report is used in evidence at a Family Court hearing, and results in the judge ruling that in all probability the father has abused his daughter. The evidence is not adequate for a criminal conviction, but the mother is given sole custody of Fay and Philip is denied access.

After years of battling with the authorities, Philip managed to obtain a copy of the interview videotape. An independent psychologist viewed the tape, and was able to demonstrate very clearly how the allegations were moulded by a combination of misleading questions, modelling and selective reinforcement. The father was cleared by a judge. However, he is still not allowed access to his child. After years of sexual abuse counselling, and living with a mother who is convinced that the abuse happened, Fay believes her father is a monster who did horrible things to her when she was little.

Recall under counselling and hypnosis

It is extremely important to someone who has been sexually abused that her experience is not denied by her therapist and others. It is her feelings about the remembered events that should be validated, however, with the understanding that this is what she believes has happened. The psychotherapist's job is not to help her retrieve lost memories. Rather it is to help her develop an understanding of her lifestory, especially those parts of it that are disempowering, and revise it in a positive way. It is her narrative and not her historical truth that is important. In this respect a therapist should believe everything yet believe nothing that a client says.

Our memories of past events, especially distant ones, are very imprecise.

Many counsellors use hypnosis to "regress" clients to an earlier period in their lives when they will presumably be able to recall events with greater clarity and detail, or to recall events that have been repressed. Some therapists use the same technique to explore "past lives".

There is no scientific data in memory research supporting this concept of memory repression. Much research in fact indicates that memories obtained under hypnosis or during psychoanalysis are seldom accurate, although they can be helpful in treatment (Spence, 1982; Orne, 1988).

This is completely counter to the beliefs of the mainstream sexual abuse industry, who are teaching therapists that memories of abuse are usually repressed, and that most women will deny or not remember that they were abused as children. Abuse textbooks for workers in the field claim that many women do not remember they were abused until they undergo therapy (Bass and Davis, 1988). It is claimed they can gain their memories through regression therapy, hypnosis, or from dreams. It expected that memories will get more and more detailed with time.

Counsellors are instructed to believe their clients have been sexually abused, even if they doubt it themselves. If a client is unsure that she was abused but thinks she might have been, the counsellor should work as though she was. If she denies it, she should be asked again later.

It is extremely unlikely that a child or an adult will enter therapy having forgotten or repressed a traumatic event such as sexual abuse (Rogers, 1992).The evidence is overwhelming that such incidents are seldom if ever blotted out of memory.

Age regression under hypnosis has been studied in detail. In one study (Orne, 1951), adult subjects were told under deep hypnosis that they were six years old. Their behaviour, handwriting and drawings were studied. Although these initially appeared "childlike", the resemblance was more apparent than real. For example, when actual pictures they had drawn at six years old were compared with regressed ones, the latter demonstrated "mature oversimplification", and had been drawn in an adult way. The regressed adult would confidently relate details which could be shown to be complete confabulations by independent checks - for instance, names and appearance of primary school teachers. Although a person may experience reliving earlier events as though they were real, this usually does not actually replicate past events (Council on Scientific Affairs, American Medical Association, 1985; O'Connell et al, 1970).

Hypnosis is defined as "believed-in imaginings". Suggestion, casual remarks and subtle cues by a hypnotist can easily, wittingly or unwittingly, create pseudomemories and confabulations. This can produce serious contamination if the recall is to be used as future evidence.

For example, hypnotherapist Martin Orne (Orne, 1983) describes a case he was involved in where a sailor had been wounded in a shooting incident. A suspect was seen by the sailor at a lineup. The victim initially said the suspect looked like the assailant, but wasn't him. However, after two hypnotic sessions, he became convinced that the suspect really was the man who attacked him. On this testimony, the man was arrested and charged with attempted murder. It was later shown, however, that he had a water-tight alibi and was completely innocent.

Pseudomemories produced under hypnosis are often totally and permanently believed in and resistant to challenge. In the above example, the sailor continued to believe the suspect was the offender, despite evidence which disproved this. Two years later he was still complaining that "a guy nearly killed me and they let him off on a technicality".

Memories recalled in counselling sessions, including under trance and hypnosis, may be very valuable to work with in therapy. It should not be assumed however that these memories necessarily record actual and accurate events. The perception and memory of later events will change one's memories of past events (Rubin, 1985). A patient's recollections in therapy will also be coloured by the therapist's questions and interpretation (Bonanno, 1990).

Parents confronted with these recovered memories usually deny that anything ever happened. As it is believed that offenders will nearly always deny their actions, however, this is seen as confirmation that the memories are actually real. I know of cases where elderly parents have been devastated by an outraged daughter angrily accusing her father of sexually molesting her in childhood. These cruel allegations, based on revelations of completely "blocked" memories, have lead to couples suffering terrible heartache and pain, sometimes even suicide (Doe, 1991).

Accuracy of clinical judgements and predictions

Sexual abuse counsellors often claim that years of experience enable them to predict when a child or adult has been sexually abused. However research shows that there is no relationship between a therapist's years of clinical experience and his or her accuracy of judgement (Dawes, 1989; Brehmer, 1980).
- Psychologists and psychiatrists seldom get feedback about how accurate their diagnoses and predictions have been.

- Clinical judgements may be "self-fulfilling prophesies". Belief in a particular outcome might greatly increase the chance of that happening. For example, if it is believed that a juvenile delinquent is likely to reoffend, that bias might influence how he or she behaves in the future.

Human beings tend to over-concentrate on information which supports their hypotheses and views of the world. Any contradictory information will be under-attended to. Mistaken beliefs or conclusions that result will generally be resistant to any further evidence that counters them (Dawes et al, 1989; Pfohl, 1979).

There is in fact clear evidence to show that an experienced clinician cannot predict whether someone has been abused, or has been an abuser, with any degree of accuracy. They will be no more accurate than a totally untrained lay-person, as has been demonstrated in a number of experiments (Dawes, 1989).

The effect of stress on witness accuracy

Sexual abuse workers often make the claim that stressful or violent events will be remembered better than neutral ones. Research however shows just the opposite. Mentally shocking events actually cause poorer recall of details, although subjects will still remember the incident occurring (Loftus and Burns, 1984; Raphael et al, 1991; Steele et al, 1980).

In Loftus and Burns' studies, subjects watched one of two versions of a film about a bank robbery, one of which involved a violent episode. Those who watched the violent version were much less accurate in reporting details of what they had seen, than those who saw the nonviolent film.

Judges have been known to express the belief that witnesses' memories are more likely to be reliable in cases of violent crime (Loftus and Burns, 1984). In fact, all available research findings indicate the opposite. There is no empirical basis for the belief held by sexual abuse workers and the legal profession, that high arousal or stress helps eyewitness accuracy (Peters, 1991).

Credibility in the courtroom

Members of a jury will tend to believe witnesses more if their evidence includes trivial details, even if these are irrelevant. Research has shown, however, that witnesses who are better are identification actually have poorer memory for peripheral details. Witnesses who offer lots of information about what they remember are in fact less likely to be accurate about the important events (Bell and Loftus, 1988). The ease by which memory can be distorted by post-event information is well known and reported in academic circles. This is not common knowledge, however, either to the legal profession, or to the general public, who are called on to serve as jurors (Kassin et al, 1989).

The nature of the judicial system is adversarial. This leads to the assumption that one party is lying, and the other telling the truth. It is clear, however, that the historical truth will often be quite different from the subjective reality of either complainant or defendant.

It is vital that courts should come to recognise the changing nature of memory. The influencing factors of time, conversations, and interviews from a range of people in authority (including health professionals, social welfare workers, counsellors and psychotherapists, police and the judiciary) should be considered when evidence relies solely on reported memories. Extreme caution should be taken before an alleged offender is convicted where there is no corroborative evidence that a distant event actually occurred.

5. What is Sexual Abuse?

"There are three kinds of lies: lies, damned lies and statistics"
Benjamin Disraeli, Autobiography, 1880.

Ten years ago, the term 'sexual abuse' was practically unheard of outside a narrow specialist group. Today, it is difficult to escape from. Every day, sexual abuse cases and issues are reported and discussed by the popular media. Various television stars and minor royalty have disclosed their awful secret to the women's magazines, to confirm that, yes, indeed, it is fashionable, and in short, the public is thoroughly involved. We certainly appear to be in the throes of a sexual abuse epidemic.

What is not generally clear, however, is what is actually meant when sexual abuse is alleged. There is in fact no one entity that is "sexual abuse", and the term is used to describe many different events by different people and agencies and in very different contexts.

The assumption that sexual abuse is a clearly definable entity underpins this field. Sexual abuse workers will often claim that it is obvious to all aware and caring adults as to what constitutes abuse. In practice, this is simply not correct. Working definitions vary widely, depending on where you are and whom you are dealing with.

Even in theory this claim is suspect. When the literature is studied, theoretical definitions of sexual abuse are seen to vary widely from study to study. Not only is this so from country to country, but even inside the same countries there exists a similar divergence (Bachmann al, 1988; Wong, 1987). This includes differing legal, behavioural and sociological definitions.

Many papers discuss studies of incidence of abuse where the diagnosis is the subjective decision of the victim and *actual events are not considered.*

Different behaviours or events are considered as wrong (immoral), illegal, or harmful by different cultures and countries at different times. Even infanticide has been considered acceptable by some cultures at some times.

From one culture and one period to another there is also disagreement about which behaviours belong under which heading. This is further complicated by a tendency for acts seen as immoral to be assumed inevitably harmful without scientific validation. How professionals deal with sexual abuse will be affected by whether they perceive it to be a crime, a sickness, or a family problem (Saunders, 1988).

Even the age that differentiates between a child and a young person, and the age of consent itself, is not universally acknowledged but varies from culture to culture and country to country. For example, the legal age of consent varies from state to state in the United States (may be up to eighteen years). It is thirteen in Japan and sixteen in New Zealand and England, although in the latter it goes up to twenty-one for homosexual acts.

The legal age of consent also varies over time. In England, it has previously been twelve years, later increased to thirteen, and is now sixteen years of age.

Some countries make a further distinction between a child and a young person. For example, in New Zealand a child is under fourteen years and a young person between the ages of fourteen and seventeen years. British law similarly distinguishes between a young girl (under thirteen) and an adolescent girl (fourteen or fifteen years old).

In many circles there has been a broadening of what sexual abuse encompasses, now including situations where a child is not actually physically touched by an adult (for example, where a child is photographed nude or able to see an adult couple having sexual intercourse).

Inconsistencies of definitions makes the comparison of results from different research studies difficult or impossible. It also renders interpretation of increased reported incidence of sexual abuse virtually meaningless. to add to the confusion in respect to definition, there is a tendency in some circles to dismiss and notions of "degrees" of sexual abuse as irrelevant. The belief is that any degree of sexual abuse may be responsible for any degree of harm, and the perpetrator is responsible for whatever happens.

A further factor is involved when studies made during the 1970s are compared with those in the late 1980s or early 1990s. A social climate predisposed to view sex as emotionally healthy and liberating - especially for women - reported little damage from sexual experience. The present social climate tends to view sex as exploitive and with explosive potential for medical, psychological and emotional damage. Not surprisingly, "research" figures are now revealing extensive damage almost wherever one cares to look.

This chapter explores some of the different ways sexual abuse is being defined in the Western world and how we can try to assess what is actually happening to children.

Legal definitions

Sexual abuse is a term seldom defined legally. Different countries have a variety of sexual crimes against children on their statutes. These include child molestation, indecent assault, sexual violation, sexual victimisation, unlawful sexual connection, sexual misuse, carnal knowledge, child rape and incest.

In some instances there will be precise definitions of what is meant by these terms. More often, however, they are inadequately specified. For instance, forty-two American states include sexual molestation in their child abuse statutes, but thirty-four of these do not even attempt to define what it is (Mrazek, 1980).

In California, child molestation is "any illegal act performed on or within the body of a child where there is lewd intent on the part of the perpetrator" (Woodling and Kossoris, 1981). In other states, it is only molestation if the perpetrator is significantly older (for instance, more than five years) than the victim.

British law defines the crime of indecent assault of a child under sixteen as an act "either inherently indecent or one that is hostile or threatening or one which the child is demonstrably reluctant to accept". What makes an act "inherently indecent" is not explained.

In New Zealand, new laws introduced in 1985 define two offences of sexual violation: unlawful sexual connection and rape. Sexual connection means the penetration of the genitals or anus of anyone by either the body of someone else, or by an object held or manipulated by anyone else. Both the offender and the victim can be either male or female. Rape is defined as "penetration of the vagina without consent and without believing on reasonable grounds, that the other person consents".

The term incest is generally reserved for sexualised contact of a child by an older family member. Other legislation includes incest as a possible crime between consenting adults, if they are related and could not be legally married (for example, sexual contact between adult brother and sister).

It can be seen that even within the confines of legal statute, there is often lack of precision as to exactly what constitutes an illegal act. There is also considerable variability between countries (or even between states) as to what behaviours are deemed against the law.

Social definitions

In North America, the term child sexual abuse commonly means sexual activity involving a child that has one of two dimensions:
- it occurs in a relationship where it is deemed exploitative by virtue of an age difference or caretaking relationship that exists with the child, or
- it occurs as the result of force or threat.

Thus, in professional and popular terms, there is almost universal agreement that sexual contact between a child and his/her parent or step-parent, older relative, teacher or baby-sitter constitutes sexual abuse. Sexual contact at the hands of any adult or significantly older person, whether known or unknown, is also sexual abuse. Rape and forced sexual contact at the hands of anyone, even a peer, is generally included.

However, not everyone uses this definition, and moreover there is not universal agreement about the exact boundaries of various terms. Some agencies define a child as under sixteen years, others up to eighteen. An exploitative age difference may be considered present if the older partner is two, four, five or more years older, depending on the location and the agency (Russell, 1983).

What constitutes sexual contact varies likewise. Intercourse and genital touching will always be included, but some definitions include acts of exposure towards children as well as actual physical touching. Child prostitution and pornography are often also included (Finkelhor, 1985; Heger, 1985; AMA 1985).

Likewise, in Britain, Canada and Australasia, social welfare and health agencies and organisations use a wide range of definitions. In New Zealand, the national Mental Health Foundation defines sexual abuse as "any sexual contact between an adult and a child. This contact can include touching and poking into the vagina, mouth, anus, or making the child touch the adult's sexual parts". The HELP Foundation, a medical and counselling service for sexual assault victims, operating in conjunction with the police, extends their definition to include "making a child look at an adult's sexual parts".

The New South Wales Child Protection Council in Australia also includes exhibitionism and suggestive behaviour in its definition of sexual assault (NSW Child Protection Council, 1985). Liz Kelly, researcher with the Child Abuse Study Unit at the North London Polytech, goes even further and includes sexual harassment and sexual comments towards children in her definition (Kelly, 1988).

Many agencies, especially counselling services, incorporate feminist analysis into their definition of sexual abuse. In this context, all sexual abuse is seen as an abuse of power. The offender is said to have more power than the child and misuses that power to take advantage of the child for his or her own sexual gratification. Children are defined as effectively powerless in the presence of adults, and any sexual contact, even an activity initiated by the child, is seen as taking advantage of the child's trust and respect. The child is not capable of consent and is never to blame for what happens.

Adults are more powerful than children, but this does not mean that children are not able to influence what happens to them in any way. Children know what feels pleasurable and what hurts. A child that squirms, struggles or cries is letting an adult know very clearly that it does not like what is happening. A child that chortles and asks for more when tickled and stroked, even if the touching includes the breast and genital areas, is unlikely to be feeling traumatised. Reframing this in later childhood or adulthood as a terrible and harmful experience is unlikely to be in a person's best interests. Great care must be taken that any intervention by a therapist or researcher does not itself cause damage.

Sociological definitions

Some workers have attempted to define sexual abuse within a social and cultural context. In the early 1960s Child Protection Worker C. Henry Kempe rediscovered child abuse and brought it to international attention (Underwager et al, 1990). In the 1970's he came up with a definition of sexual abuse, various versions of which are still quoted by some organisations and professionals today (Schechter and Roberge, 1976; Kempe, 1978; Krugman, 1986; Turvill, 1986; Bentovim, 1987). This definition attempts to explain sexual activities of children within their social and cultural contexts, and can be described as follows:

Sexual abuse is the involvement of dependent developmentally immature children and young people in sexual activities they cannot fully understand, to which they cannot give informed consent and which violate the social taboos of the culture and are against the law.

Lip service is often paid to considering sexual activities in the context of what is considered acceptable behaviour within a specific subculture. Generally, however, the different behaviours and mores of a minority culture are ignored and Western society imposes its beliefs and values on these groups. What is considered morally acceptable in different cultures will be further explored in the next chapter.

Retrospective definitions

There is a basic conflict between saying some particular behaviour is always harmful (and hence abusive), and looking at the effects of a specific event and claiming that it was abusive because some harm has been shown to have occurred subsequently. Some definitions of abuse specify certain behaviours as always damaging. Others look at the context in which the event occurred, the perceived intent of the alleged offender, and the psychological outcome of what happened. Some agencies are concentrating solely on the later effects of past events, and defining abuse retrospectively.

There are dangers of specifying certain behaviours as always harmful. For instance, defining an adult touching a child's genitals as sexual abuse does not take into account care giving activities such as changing nappies and washing bottoms, or when necessary for medical examination and treatment.

Much of the current research into sexual abuse either does not precisely define what it is measuring, or it uses retrospective definitions. This means that something is defined as abusive if an adult (usually a woman) believes that she experienced any sexual act as a child or adolescent that she now believes was harmful to her. This is irrespective as to whether it caused her any discomfort or anxiety at the time.

There have been several prevalence studies using this sort of definition (Brant and

Tisva, 1977; von Dadzelszen, 1986; Mullen et at, 1988). These surveys describe very broad definitions, for example "..any unwanted or negative sexual experience in childhood and/or early adolescence". Some surveys simply ask whether the respondent ever experienced sexual abuse as a child, without even defining the term (Kelly, 1988; Mullens et al, 1991).

Studies involving questionnaires asking for a history of abuse in this way come up with a very large number of respondents claiming abuse. Figures are widely quoted that "one in three or four" girls are sexually abused, and "one in ten" boys. While these will certainly include many cases where children have suffered exploitative abusive sexual acts from adults, there is a real danger in interpreting figures obtained this way.

There are a number of reasons why figures can be grossly inflated and distorted by retrospective surveys.

Firstly, in many studies, data includes cases where children were bathed by adults in a way they now feel was unpleasant, witnessed their parents having sexual intercourse, or saw their parents walk naked around the home. Including cases of 'bad touching' (for example, a child being kissed or hugged by an adult and deciding that this was 'yukky') can also greatly inflate the statistics (Money, 1991).

There is also a current trend for women to recall childhood memories in therapy that they now believe were unpleasant or harmful. Given the understanding of how these memories are reconstructed, as explained in the last chapter, it can be seen that relying on such information could falsely magnify the reported incidence of abuse.

Although what is called sexual abuse often involves actions in this grey area - inappropriate sensual touching or kissing, for instance - this is not the impression given by the media. Generally it is the worst sort of abuse that is portrayed - the public are saturated with images of the menacing molester and the cowering, terrified little girl.

The implication is that this is sexual abuse, and this is what is happening to one in three of our girls.

Likewise, the teaching material for workers tends to concentrate on these worst-case scenarios. They will extrapolate the effects on these victims onto those who have experienced minor inappropriate actions in the context of a loving relationship, so that counsellors are trained to believe in and expect the worst kind of damage whether it exists or not.

Definition difficulties

Everyone is likely to agree that genital contact between adults and children involving force or coercion is sexual abuse. Broadening a definition beyond this, however, means each case requires complex judgements as to whether it is abusive.

This includes looking at the *context* of what is taking place. Touching a child's genitals may be for hygiene or health reasons. Seeing a man exposing his penis by 'flashing' in a park may be different for a child from seeing father naked in the bathroom. Further, children who are accustomed to family nudity may well respond differently to the flasher from children who have never seen adult naked bodies or genitals.

The *intent* on behalf of the adult needs to be considered. For instance, consider the scenario of a little girl touching or playing with her father's penis while they shower together. Some agencies define this as abusive under any circumstances (Rosenfeld et al, 1986). If the touching is directed and encouraged by the father for his own sexual stimulation, most people in Western cultures would consider this inappropriate and exploitative.

However, children are curious about bodies and will tend to touch their own and others, without differentiating between sexual and non sexual parts. Touching daddy's penis is likely to be part of this exploratory process. It might even be incidental contact from the close physical proximity of sharing a shower. Many parents will view such events as part of natural curiosity. They may take the opportunity to teach the child about sexual matters appropriate to their age. This might include where and when it is acceptable to touch other people.

Clearly, the scenario where a little girl initiates the touch through her own curiosity is very different from the one where her father encourages her to masturbate him. The intent of the adult concerned is however often not taken into account. Some agencies work with the definition that even one episode of a child having touched a parent's genitals means sexual abuse. If all the children who did this were removed from their homes, we would clearly have a lot fewer children growing up with their parents.

The *effect* of behaviours also needs to be looked at. Unfortunately, assessing whether a particular childhood event will cause a child any trouble later in life is very difficult and complicated. As mentioned above, for one child, seeing a 'flasher' might be very frightening and traumatic. For another, it might have been a very minor incident.

The trend is growing for adults who recall sexual incidents as children to see them as having been traumatic in the light of their adult values and beliefs. The event at the time might have not appeared abusive or unpleasant to the child. This is the stand encouraged by many sexual abuse therapists. It is a circular argument: because all adult/child sexual contact is harmful, any such experiences were abusive, and the therapy will help develop this realisation.

Certainly studies indicate that children suffering serious ongoing incest are more likely to develop psychological and social problems such as depression, alcohol abuse or prostitution (Wourtele et al, 1990; Kiser et al, 1991; Margo and McLees, 1991; Pribor and Dinwiddie, 1992; Scott 1992). However great care should be taken when looking retrospectively at the effects of early sexual experiences. Deciding that they are inevitably detrimental can be a self-fulfilling prophecy.

There is no doubt that children thrive with loving hugs and cuddles. They enjoy kisses, strokes and tickles. Experiencing love and affection through physical contact is essential for their healthy development (Stecher, 1980). There is a very grey area between loving sensuality and abusive sexuality. Behaviours which are socially condoned and developmentally necessary are very close to those which are socially forbidden and developmentally harmful. Undressing children, washing them and helping them go to the toilet inevitably involves a certain amount of touching the genital area by the parents. It is extremely difficult, if not impossible, for a child to differentiate between contact that is associated with sexual arousal on the adult's part and contact that is not (Gardner, 1992).

What is acceptable is very open to interpretation. Sexual abuse workers' moral and political beliefs can influence what they decide is abusive. When they include non-specified 'bad touching', seeing naked adults and being able to witness adults having sexual intercourse, they cross the line of what is considered acceptable in many families.

Sadly, many adults, especially men, are now very cautious about having physical contact with children. There is a growing fear that gestures of affection or comfort might be construed or distorted as sexual abuse. Many teachers are becoming wary of cuddling children who hurt themselves in the playground. Child-care workers are instructed to never be alone with a child. Fathers are worried about hugging their daughters. Men keep their distance from their relatives' and friends' children whom they would previously have touched and kissed affectionately.

We have reached an era when a significant percentage of men are prepared to contribute substantially in the care of their children. Ironically, more and more are now feeling scared that changing babies' nappies and bathing them leaves them vulnerable to allegations of sexual abuse.

Interpretation of statistics

There has been a manyfold increase in the reported incidence of sexual abuse in the past one to two decades. Incidence can be defined as the number of new cases occurring during a certain period. Prevalence is the number of cases in existence at a certain time within a given area.

It is clear that genuine cases were under-reported in the past, when there was a general climate of ignorance and denial about the problem. What is not clear is whether the frequency of abuse has actually increased, or just that these figures reflect that more people are either spontaneously disclosing abuse or revealing it through therapy.

Certainly there is an epidemic of alleged offences. As has been shown, however, the broadening of the definition has expanded the abuse statistics. Current prevalence figures suggest that a range from 6% to 66% of girls and 3% to 31% of boys are sexually abused (Bachmann et al, 1988; Lecky, 1991; Watkins and Bentovim, 1992). A recent New Zealand study states that 33% of women report abuse as girls (Mullen, 1991).

The most common figures quoted in the media today are that one in three or four girls and one in nine or ten boys are sexually abused (Saphira, 1985; Herbert 1985).

These figures need to be interpreted with caution. They may include cases where memories are recalled of events that did not occur. They may also include those who now reinterpret their childhood experiences as harmful. They also include many cases where the story is confabulated and declared unfounded in court. The sexual abuse industry will usually continue to believe in the validity of the claim even when the accused is acquitted, and these cases remain as part of the sexual abuse statistics.

If people who have grown up in a sexually permissive culture are later confronted by a culture or era that is sexually oppressive, they face a severe challenge to their values and belief systems. They may become convinced that their earlier experiences were abusive and damaging, and have to deal with feelings of guilt and shame, and anger and bitterness towards their alleged offender. By emphasising the probable trauma they have sustained, the intervention process significantly contributes to the victim's sense of being seriously damaged.

In 1964, before there was a high level of public and professional awareness and suspicion of sexual abuse, the reported New Zealand incidence of incest was only one in one million, although the actual incidence was estimated to be about five per million ((Medlicott, 1967). Although this is likely to be an under-estimation, in the last thirty years the perceived incidence of abuse has increased by more than one million percent.

The effects of defining a third of our female population as victims of sexual abuse, and a third of our males as offenders, should be seriously considered. If this is truly the case, then we are defining very common human activities as bad and harmful.

We are also teaching an entire generation that this is common practice. It is certainly possible that such messages constantly emphasised by the media will encourage boys and men to reason that if so many others are doing it, why should not they?

The projected financial cost of providing ongoing counselling for all these victims and prison sentences for even a minor percentage of the offenders is astronomical. There is also a huge social and emotional price in a third of girls growing up to believe they have been permanently damaged by men. Experiencing retribution through the legal system is seldom a positive process for our men. This leads to a very large percentage of our population defined as criminals. New Zealand already has the greatest number of people imprisoned per head of population in the Western world. If we do verify the statistics put forward by the sexual abuse industry, we will never have the resources to respond adequately to all these crimes.

In my estimate, these figures actually represent a combination of all the following scenarios and more:

- sexual acts with a child involving force or threats of violence
- similar acts involving coercion and secrecy
- consensual sexual contact between a child and adult
- consensual sexual acts between a teenager and an adult
- minor sexual acts between child and adult such as inappropriate touching
- cases where affectionate touches or bathing a child are misinterpreted as sexual
- custody cases, often where the child becomes convinced she was abused when nothing has happened
- false allegations of satanic abuse and sex rings, often arising from interviewing children in day-care centres
- post-event recall by adults in therapy or under hypnosis
- other retrospective adult recall of unwanted childhood sexual experiences with adults
- retrospective recall of childhood events involving peers.

We are certainly experiencing a sexual abuse epidemic. It is vital that we go beyond the hysteria and look at just what we mean by this, and the implications of defining the world in this way.

6. Childhood Sexuality

"There is nothing either good or bad, but thinking makes it so."
William Shakespeare, Hamlet, Act II Scene II.

All forms of human sexual activity have been condoned or admired in certain places at certain times. Masturbation, incest and bestiality have all been considered healthy or praiseworthy in some cultures, and sinful or unhealthy in others. Historically, Western society has had very different attitudes to childhood sexual activities than we have today.

Historical review of adult/child sex

In early Greek and Roman civilisations, sexual love between adult men and young boys was acceptable and even idealised. Brothels of boy prostitutes were established and there was even castration of some male babies to improve their later attraction as prostitutes.

In Medieval Europe, sexual matters were not hidden from children. Families often slept together in a single room, and children would witness their parents having sexual intercourse. It was common for children to be the subject of coarse jokes and sexual gestures, and have their genitals fondled by adults (Schultz, 1982). Adults routinely masturbated babies to soothe them and put them to sleep.

It was expected that boys and girls should have sex as soon as they had physically matured. No-one took offence at Dante's love for nine year old Beatrice (Brongersma, 1988). In England in the sixteenth century, thirteen year old Elizabeth Ramsbotham made an official complaint that she had not yet been deflowered by her eleven year old husband, John Bridge. In the same era, the Dutch painter and scholar Carel van Mander taught his twelve year old boy students to have sex in order to prevent headaches.

One of the best illustrations of the European attitude to child sexuality in the early seventeenth century is the story of young Louis XIII of France's sexual activities, which were recorded in a diary by Henry IV's physician, Heroard. When he was one, Louis would show adults his penis, ask them to kiss it, and get his nanny to play with it. The courtiers were amused to see his first erections and would tease him sexually. He would pretend "to give you all some milk from my cock" and play that it was a drawbridge, "raising and lowering it". This joking stopped when he reached seven and he was considered to be a little man. At fourteen he was married and encouraged or even pressured to perform sexually with his wife (Aries, 1962).

During Medieval times child marriages were common in nearly all European countries (Fielding, 1961). In Scotland premature marriages reached such numbers that in 1600 they were forbidden, and the minimum age limit set to twelve years for females and fourteen for males. Early marriage was also common in Renaissance France and Italy. Children of distinguished families were often betrothed at two or three years old.

The idea of childhood did not exist in the Middle Ages. From between five to seven years of age, children entered the community where they worked and played as adults. The notion of childhood developed in the seventeenth and eighteenth centuries amongst the bourgeoisie, who could afford the luxury of coddling their children.

Moralists in the seventeenth century began to regard children as requiring both protection and reforming. Separate bedrooms and beds for children were advocated, although these did not become common until the Victorian era. As part of the process of differentiating "children" from "adults", children were to be protected from crude language and actions, and from seeing nudity or intercourse. Boys were subjected to strict discipline through their years of schooling before entering the 'freedom' of adulthood (Parton, 1985). The world witnessed a trend prohibiting all pre-pubertal sexual expression.

Sexual exploitation of children was first recognised legally in Britain in the mid-sixteenth century. In 1548 a law was passed protecting boys from forced sodomy and in 1576 one protecting girls under ten from forced rape (Wakefield et al, 1988). In the last three centuries, the age of consent has been progressively increased to twelve, thirteen and now sixteen years in Britain (and stands at twenty-one years for homosexual acts). In America, the age of consent has reached eighteen years in some States.

The campaign to stamp out childhood masturbation developed in the eighteenth century, as described earlier. It was considered the responsibility of adults to make children feel guilty about sexual self-stimulation. Parents were advised to speak and act towards children in a chaste manner and punish any masturbation severely. Children were considered to be sexually dangerous and adults were required to act forcefully to maintain a child's asexuality.

The use of retraining devices and surgical intervention reached its height near the end of the nineteenth century. By the 1920s, it was becoming recognised that masturbation did not cause the paediatric problems attributed to it. These days it is largely acknowledged that masturbation does not result in physical harm, yet a moral judgement against it still prevails in many sectors of our society.

This century has witnessed the evolution of adolescence as a developmental stage in social maturity. As the duration of education has extended, and the marriageable age increased, young people have remained under the care of their parents for much longer periods of time. This has resulted in the phenomenon of teenagers, young people between the ages of thirteen and nineteen who are sexually mature but who have not yet taken on the full social responsibilities of adulthood. Adolescence is now a significant social force, with a major impact on consumer markets.

Anthropological studies

Examination of the sexual practices of some non-Western cultures is even more revealing. Anthropological studies reveal human cultures ranging from the sexually repressive, which prohibit all non-procreative sex, to the sexually-permissive, which tolerate or encourage sexual activity at all ages. Ford and Beach (1951) describe a number of societies where childhood sexual activities have been commonplace. As indigenous people have come in contact with European culture and values this century, their individual cultural practices have been increasingly modified towards Western attitudes.

Some societies have actively stimulated their babies and young children. Hopi and Siriono parents frequently masturbated their children. Kazak adults would stimulate small children's genitals, especially boys, when playing with them. In Alorese society, mothers would fondle their babies' genitals whilst breast feeding. Alorese boys would masturbate openly and sometimes attempt intercourse with little girls.

In the Polynesian society of Pukapuka, both boys and girls would masturbate freely in public without adult censure. A similar situation existed with the Trobiand Islanders, whose girls and boys would also openly engage in sexual games including mutual masturbation, oral sex and simulated intercourse (Ford and Beach, 1951).

The Chewa of Africa believed that children would not be able to have offspring of their own unless they were sexually practised from childhood. Older children would build little huts outside of the village, where boys and girls would play at being husbands and wives with the full support of their parents. There would be periodic exchange of partners. Sometimes these practice-marriages would continue until marriage, which took place at adolescence.

Likewise, the little children of the North-West Melanesians would build secluded huts and play husband and wife games, which would include imitating the act of sex. By the age of six to eight for girls, and ten to twelve for boys, the children would have active sex lives. Adults would show a tolerant and amused interest, gossiping about the little love affairs of their children (Malinowski, 1929).

The Ifugao head hunters of the Philippines had similar practices. In this society, older children and adolescents slept together in dormitories until marriage. It was expected for the boys to sleep with a girl each night, and they were encouraged to be sexually active by their fathers. The frequent swapping of partners was imposed by the girl, who was usually unwilling to form too prolonged an attachment to a boy until she was ready to be married, which was generally soon after puberty. In the occasional event that a girl became pregnant before marriage, one of her lovers was expected to marry her.

Amongst the Muria, a non-Hindu tribal people of the Central India hill country, unmarried young people would similarly sleep together in dormitories, called ghotul. Children would be encouraged to spend time in the ghotul by about the time they reached six. Although they would not be expected to have sexual relations immediately, they would be exposed to the sexual activities of the older children, and would gradually become more confident and experienced sexually. The girls' headmistress would decide who slept with whom, and generally constant partner-swapping was encouraged. Forming an attachment to a sexual partner was frowned upon, as marriage plans were usually decided by the older generation (Constantine and Martinson, 1980).

The Lepcha of India believed that girls needed to have intercourse to mature. Sex play amongst their children involved mutual masturbation and attempted intercourse. Most girls would be having full sexual intercourse regularly at eleven or twelve years of age. Occasionally adult men would copulate with girls as young a eight years. Such behaviour was completely condoned by the Lepcha.

Some cultures have routinely practised adult-child homosexuality. All men and boys of the Siwa Valley, North Africa, were reported to engage in anal intercourse. Men were seen as peculiar if they did not do so, and would lend each other their sons for this purpose. In the Aranda Aboriginal society of Central Australia, fully-initiated unmarried men would take boys aged ten or twelve to live with them as their wives for several years, until the older men married. The Kiwai men of New Guinea also practised sodomy, which they believed gave their young men strength.

The Telugu-speaking people of central southern India have certain genital-touching practices which persist today (Money et al, 1991). Girls are unclothed until they are two, and boys remain naked until they are six. From infancy until aged six, the children are frequently kissed, hugged and fondled by adults. Fathers and other male relatives will greet a little boy by lifting him until his genital region is at mouth level and then kissing his penis. After the boy is six, this gesture changes. The man flicks or pulls the boy's foreskin with his thumb and the first three fingers of his right hand. Then he lifts his bunched fingers to his lips, makes a kissing sound, and throws the kiss back to the penis. He might repeat this two or three times. If the man is a visitor, such as an uncle, this is an act of greeting. The visitor comes up to the boy, puts his left hand around the boy's upper arm, and carries out the penis gesture with his right hand. This salutation is an act of homage.

Girls of the same age do not receive a similar act of homage from their female kinsfolk. A woman visitor of lower social rank may however touch a young girl's genitals with bunched fingers, raise them to her lips and throw back a kiss of homage to the girl's superior social status. The meaning of these acts is neither erotic nor sexual, although in contemporary America and elsewhere these behaviours would be defined as sexually abusive. These behaviours are precursors to healthy sexological maturity within the context of Telugu culture. It would be inappropriate to impose on this culture the Western belief that any adult manual contact with the genitopelvic region of a child other than hygienic care is sexual abuse.

It can be seen that human cultures vary vastly, geographically and over time, in their degree of acceptance of sex. This ranges from repressive and restrictive to permissive and supportive, and includes varying degrees of acceptance of sexual activities between children and adults ((Marshall and Suggs, 1971; Constantine and Martinson, 1981). Many actions considered abusive in modern Western society, such as masturbation of children by parents, and sexual initiation at puberty, have been regarded as normal by other cultures and in other ages (West, 1988).

Sexuality of children

The concept of children as being asexual and innocent was first developed in the second half of the eighteenth century. An asexual child can have no sexual impulses and hence would never desire sexual contact. It therefore follows that all sexual contact would be initiated by indecent men against innocent children, who could never be held responsible for any sexualised behaviour.

Scientific theory since Freud, and social research since Kinsey, has demonstrated very clearly that from the earliest age, children are sexual beings, they are interested and excited by sex (Langford, 1991; Constantine and Martinson, 1981; Masters and Johnson, 1970; Kinsey et al, 1948 and 1953).

Children have sexual feelings from birth and may spontaneously begin sex play at very young age. Babies less than a year old have been observed to masturbate. Kinsey (1948) estimated that more than half of all boys could masturbate to orgasm by the age of three to four, and almost all could do so three to four years before reaching puberty. It is in fact common for children to start rubbing their sexual organs as soon as they have sufficiently developed their hand and arm co-ordination. This behaviour is spontaneous and not learned, and will sometimes but not always result in orgasm (Constantine, 1980).

Children reared in sexually permissive societies will readily engage in sex play from infancy. Children growing up in an environment where adult sexual activities are not hidden, will imitate these behaviours with their peers and also with adults. Children touch and imitate as part of their normal exploratory behaviour (Rosenfeld et al, 1986).

In contrast to many primitive people and inhabitants of ancient non-European empires, our modern civilisation is guilt-ridden about sex. Some Christian teachings claim that sex is root of all evil, as illustrated by the story of Adam and Eve's original sin in the Garden of Eden. Whilst not necessarily bound by the rules of the Church, the West still passes on the message to children that "sex is dangerous".

Children learn that sex is something not to be talked about - they see adults being awkward, secretive, changing the subject, or viewing it as unpleasant and dirty. Adults transmit their anxieties about sex to children. In the current climate, a child's earliest education in sexual matters is likely to be about sexual abuse. Children are taught about "yukky touching" and how children can be harmed by sexual contact, and this message is seldom balanced with messages of the pleasure and intimacy to be obtained from sexual contact in loving adult relationships.

As mentioned above, there have been many cultures where sex play amongst children has been encouraged. In Micronesia, Africa and some parts of India, children and young teenagers were allowed free sexual contact in adolescent "club houses". Small children were initiated into sexual life by older adolescents. Studies have indicated that children growing up under these conditions exhibited no social stigmatisation and appeared to suffer no adverse psychological sequelae. Researcher Verrier Elwin studied the Muria people extensively, and published seventeen volumes of ethnographic data. He concluded that the Muria had an exceptionally high rate of stable and happy marriages, with a divorce rate of only 3% (compared with an American divorce rate of 50% in 1975).

Other studies have indicated that many childhood sexual behaviours and experiences may be harmless per se (Leitenberg et al, 1989; Constantine and Martinson, 1981; Schultz and Jones, 1983; Li et al, 1990). In one study, adult functioning of women with sexual experiences in childhood was assessed (Kilpatrick, 1986). These women showed no differences with respect to self-esteem, depression, marital and sexual satisfaction, and family relations, from those with no childhood sexual experiences. Sexual experiences that were forced, guilt-producing, harmful or pressured, were however related to detrimental adult functioning.

In 1983 Dr Michael Baurrmann reported the results of an enormous study he carried out for the German police. This study assessed 8,058 young people (more boys than girls) who had been involved in illegal sexual relationships. They found that in many cases no emotional or physical harm was sustained. Not one of the 1,000 boys under the age of fourteen years was found to be harmed. Harm to the girls, when it occurred, was sometimes (not always) a result of the sex act itself, and sometimes the result of heavy handedness by police, parents and others in the aftermath.

In 1981 in Holland, Dr Theo Sandfort published an intensive study of twenty-five pairs of boys and men involved in acknowledged sexual friendships. He found that the boys showed no signs of harm and concluded that children who have consensual sexual experiences with adults experience no bad effects later.

Another study (Nelson, 1986) of self-reports of incest (a non-patient, non-offender sample of individuals) showed that both exploitative and non exploitative experiences were perceived by some participants as negative and by others as positive. There are many other reports of women who have had sexual encounters with their fathers in childhood and not considered them damaging.

This in no way condones or advocates sexual activities between children and adults in our society. Such activities are clearly unacceptable within our current culture. The fact that a child's behaviour or conversation is sexual does not mean that an adult should respond sexually. Children need to be gently and sensitively taught appropriate behaviours without being made to believe they have done something wrong.

Children's sexual rights

There is a power differential in all relationships. With children, great power differences play a role in their relationships with parents, teachers, and even their peers. Sexual relationships are situations where people place their trust in others and expose their vulnerability, and this is especially true between children and adults. The potential for exploitation of a child is particularly high in these circumstances.

It is a mistake to make the assumption that children are completely powerless, however. Even tiny babies are able to communicate whether they are experiencing pleasure or pain. Children can let us know very clearly whether they like or dislike what is happening to them, although obviously they will not always be able to prevent harmful situations occurring.

The mainstream belief in the sexual abuse field is that children are never able to consent to any sexual acts under any circumstance. There are however other opinions regarding the issue of consent.

In the 1960s and 1970s there emerged a variety of groups with radical beliefs regarding children's sexual rights. This included the Paedophile Information Exchange (PIE) organised in Britain, which asserted that children should have some say in what they do with their own bodies and that they should be free to decide, as a matter of right, whether or not they want a sexual relationship.

The Rene Guyon Society in the United states believed that many social ills and personal emotional dysfunctioning were due to distorted attitudes to sexuality. This society actively encouraged childhood sexuality, including adult-child sex, with the motto 'sex by eight, or it's too late'. In the late 1970s an organisation called the North American Man/Boy Love Association (NAMBA) organised large-scale public conferences to address issues such as the age of consent (O'Carroll, 1980).

In conjunction with this, there were at that time a wide variety of counter-culture activities, including many sexually uninhibited communes.

These organisations largely expressed the belief that what was important was whether the child was willing to take part in the activity in question, and that unwilling children should never be subjected to sexual acts. There was no need for the child to know the 'consequences' of engaging in harmless (especially non-penetrative) sex play, simply because it was exactly that: harmless.

As would be expected, these societies have mostly been disbanded or outlawed in the sexually repressive 1980s and 1990s.

The concept of children being able to consent to sexual activity has also discussed by less radical groups and individuals, however. Even feminist writer Kate Millett (1991) believes that one of children's essential rights is to express themselves sexually. Dutch judge Edward Brongersma (1988) claims that consent does not require understanding but rather willingness that something should take place.

Finkelhor, on the other hand, argues against children's rights of sexual expression. He believes that a child can never give consent, because in his view consent requires a person understanding what he or she is consenting to, and being free to say yes or no.

The principle of individual rights is a relatively new one in the history of humanity. In ancient times no distinction was made between legal and moral - both were decided by same authority, the divine king.

In 1789 the world saw the birth of the first democracy with the overthrow of the French monarch. Leaders of the French Revolution claimed sovereign power for the people and declared that a state should not impose a particular system of morals or religion on its people. A democracy separates the authority of state and religion; the former operates by determining what is illegal, the latter decides what is immoral. There is a basic commitment of justice for everyone: all citizens are supposed to be entitled to a fair trial as defined by the laws of the land.

Within a democratic nation however, there is freedom to choose one's religious beliefs and personal moral code. Penal laws are designed to protect individuals and society from harm, not to impose morals. Some people freely accept restrictions imposed by their religious beliefs or their personal concepts of decency.

In the early nineteenth century, the United States Declaration of Independence recognised the rights of all people to life, liberty and pursuit of happiness. This is taken to include freedom of speech and freedom of religious belief. It can also be seen to be the right to sexual liberty unless one's actions are inflicting harm on others.

The concept of rights for children really only emerged in the 1970s. Since a prolonged period of childhood first emerged in the seventeenth century, there has been a tradition of secluding and protecting children from adult exploitation. This process has expanded this century with the United Nations Declaration of the Rights of the Child. This states that children have a moral right to welfare (nutrition, medical services, housing and education) and protection from abuse.

Some writers argue that children should also have certain rights usually reserved for adults, which would give them greater independence from parents before reaching the age of majority (Franklin, 1986). These range from issues such as choosing what they eat, the length they wear their hair and what TV they watch, to rights such as voting, driving, drinking alcohol, working and marrying. Although human beings do not all develop and mature at the same age, arbitrary age limits are generally set for some of these rights.

It has been suggested that children's sexual rights should include freedom from sexual exploitation, the right to express their sexuality, and the right to a comprehensive age-appropriate sex education (Richard Ives in 'The Rights of Children', Franklin, 1986). Ives argues that denying children's sexuality makes the transition from childhood through adolescence to adulthood all the more difficult.

Teenage sexual activity, mainly with peers, is widespread throughout the world. Prohibition seldom prevents their sexual experimentation, and therefore sex education should include practical information about protection from pregnancy, sexually transmitted disease and other harm. In New Zealand over 50% of young people are sexually active before the age of sixteen.

This means that in essence the law illegalising sexual behaviour under the age of 16 years is one that the majority of the population disobeys. The implications of such an unenforceable law should be considered. It could be argued that one consequence of this could be young people not growing up to be law abiding and respectful of society's rules.

It is often claimed that sexual activity with one's peers is less likely to involve exploitation than sex with adults, because an age disparity will increase the power imbalance. Some sexual reformers of the 1960s and 1970s made the opposite argument however, believing that an experienced man could be a gentler sexual initiator for a young woman than a sexually ill-educated, over-confident and insensitive teenage boy. Early teenage sex between peers is in fact often associated with poor or non-existent contraception, alcohol, drugs and sexually transmitted disease. Ultimately the dialogue returns to whether it is believed that all adult-child sexual contact is inevitably harmful.

Constantine (1981) believes that what determines a harmful contact depends on the child's knowledge and understanding of what is happening and his or her feeling of free consent based on that knowledge. Harm depends on the nature of the experience, whether it is violent, the sexual awareness of the child, the stability of his or her relationship, and most importantly, the reaction of adults when they find out about the contact.

Secondary victimisation and iatrogenic abuse

There is considerable evidence that many children are much more emotionally traumatised by the questioning and reaction which follows disclosure than by the actual sexual encounter (Constantine, 1981; Franklin, 1986). The process of intervention may often cause secondary victimisation. The emotional reactions of parents and interviewing by people in authority may result in children becoming victims because adults expect them to (Wakefield and Underwager, 1988). The possibility of long term harmful effects of any intervention should always be considered (Zeitlin, 1987; Yates 1987; Landwirth, 1987).

The primary tenet of the medical profession is "first do no harm". Practitioners must be constantly aware of the potential for iatrogenic damage. Nelson (1986) believes that this effect will be minimised if professionals and society define exploitation as actual harm done at the time. She believes that the assumption that an age difference is automatically damaging leads to a high likelihood of a child suffering iatrogenic abuse. When fear produces witch hunts for sexual abusers, there is a significant danger of one form of abuse being replaced by another (Mullen, 1991).

Damage from intervention is not just confined to the investigation of children. Counsellors who convince their clients that sexual activities they experienced as OK or enjoyable as children were really very bad and therefore harmful, are not promoting their clients' mental health.

Child sex offenders

A recent phenomenon is the rising incidence of children being labelled sex offenders, abusing other children. This used to be largely adolescent boys sexually harassing younger children, but more recently very small children, even as young as two years, have been accused of sexually molesting others.

Certainly children who have been seriously sexually abused themselves may exhibit sexually inappropriate behaviour with others. Also, children who have undergone disclosure interviews for sexual abuse often have sexual behaviours selectively reinforced by this process. Many children have only demonstrated sexualised behaviours subsequent to interrogation, especially when they have been subjected to multiple interviews.

These children often learn that sexual talk and play, as well as violent acts such as stamping or thumping "daddy" dolls or models, is rewarded by attention and praise for being "brave". When the children involved in many of the day care investigations are studied (see Chapter 9), it is apparent that they usually only develop sexual posturing and molesting other children after the investigation has started.

Although we should try to protect our children from harmful influences and stop them being abused, it is neither desirable nor realistic to protect them from everything all the time. Experiences of conflict can be painful but growthful - children learn from their mistakes. Very few people would complete their teenage years without some form of conflict or pain related to their sexuality.

If it is acknowledged that children are sexual beings, it can be seen that observing sexual activity in children should not lead to the automatic assumption that they have been sexually abused.

7. Some Specific Directions the Sexual Abuse Industry is Taking Us

"The road to hell is paved with good intentions."

The commitment to "believe children" is having some far-reaching effects and impinging on the lives of many families. Even the faintest suspicion of abuse can lead to interrogation of children by social workers - prolonged and repeated interviews up to three hours in length. These counsellors have been trained to suspend their disbelief, and operate from the premise that all the children referred to them have been abused, but will probably be too scared to tell. Many of these situations result in false allegations of abuse being made against someone, most often the child's father. This process has already been explored in previous chapters.

Children who disclose abuse in this way tend to give more and more detailed information as the interviews continue. When they perceive that the interviewer is not happy with their replies, they try harder to say whatever they think is expected of them. In some cases, they start to name other adults and children. More and more children are then caught up in the process, until highly elaborate and often contradictory stories emerge of bizarre and horrendous events.

There have been literally thousands of such incidents, some of which have attracted international media attention. Fuelled by the media, there is now a public belief that appalling sexual abuse of children in groups is widespread. Looking at these cases it is apparent that there are some very striking parallels. Many of the group allegations fall into very specific categories. In particular, there is a belief in:
- the involvement of "sex rings" in preschool
- a conspiracy of satanic cults ritually abusing children
- sexual abuse of children in alternative communities
- manufacture and distribution of child pornography on a massive scale.

Whilst it is possible there are a few isolated occasions where such allegations are founded, there is overwhelming evidence that the bulk of these allegations stem solely from the subjective belief by a professional that a child has been abused, and the subsequent interventions. Good people operating with the best of intentions are having devastating effects on some children and their families.

This chapter presents some of the more typical or famous examples of these cases.

Child day-care cases

The most famous and sensational of these cases have occurred in the United States, but similar cases are now occurring in other parts of the world, including Britain, Australia and New Zealand.

Most of these cases follow what is now a very familiar pattern. Initially, a child attending the centre presents with a problem behaviour. As previously discussed, nearly every form of problem behaviour is listed as an "indicator of sexual abuse". This behaviour leads a parent or someone in authority to suspect that the child has probably been sexually abused. Alternatively, the child may be referred for "expert" evaluation of the problem, by someone who routinely suspects sexual abuse as the prime factor in problem behaviour. Interrogating the child will usually result in denial, but this may be seen to confirm the diagnosis, as children are believed to be too scared to tell and need lots of encouragement to do so.

Eventually, this encouragement results in the child revealing abuse. Ongoing disclosure interviews, using leading questioning and selective reinforcement, result in the child giving more and more details of increasingly perverse and bizarre events. Other children and adults become implicated, until stories develop of "sex rings". Classically, the stories start to include details such as activities involving the children naked in a circle, and making them eat faeces or drink urine. Sometimes it is even claimed that the children have to watch babies or animals being sacrificed or practise cannibalism. There are often claims of the adults being dressed as witches or monsters, or wearing masks. It is believed that they sexually violate the children with fingers, mouths or genitals in every conceivable orifice. Often it is claimed that the adults take photographs or videotape these events.

The allegations and numbers of suspects begin to mount only after the investigators and child abuse agency workers enter the scene, and both parents and children become convinced of the reality of the abuse.

Usually, the majority of the children will have been presenting as well-adjusted to their parents and others, giving no indication that they were actually suffering terrible ongoing abuse. It is only after the events are 'disclosed' that many of these children start to develop signs of emotional distress, such as nightmares, aggression and sometimes inappropriate sexual behaviour.

Despite extensive investigations, none of these claims have ever been objectively verified - no props or clothes discovered, no pornography found, and no record of any babies murdered. However, even in cases where the alleged offenders are acquitted, most of the children, their families and the sexual abuse investigators, remain convinced that the abuse really did happen. The lack of evidence just confirms how fiendishly clever the abusers are.

What follows is a summary of some of the most publicised of these cases, but there are several hundred smaller but similar examples to be found in North America, Europe and Australasia (Coleman, 1989).

It should be noted that the closure of day cares is often one of the stated aims of fundamentalist religious groups, who believe that a woman's place should be in the home, raising her family and looking after her husband. At the end of the Second World War, many governments had a policy of restricting daycare facilities, requiring women to leave the workforce and make way for the employment of returning servicemen. In the current climate of unemployment in the Western world, it is again expedient to force women from the workplace. Both religious and political agendas are likely to contribute to the child care hysteria.

The Virginia McMartin Preschool, California.

This case started when a woman named Judy Johnson apparently found blood on the anus of her two year old son when collecting him from the pre-school. Examination by the emergency room at UCLA reported signs of sodomy and Ray Buckley, one of the daycare workers, was charged with sexual molestation of the child.

All the parents of over one hundred children enrolled at the preschool were contacted in writing, telling them Ray Buckley was under investigation and asking them to report any suspicions that their own children might have been abused.

The police investigated the complaint in August 1983 but got nowhere. The child was then interviewed by Kee MacFarlane, sexual abuse expert at the Children's Institute International in November 1983. MacFarlane claimed that the child disclosed that he had been abused (Wakefield and Underwager, 1992). However, the police believed that there was insufficient evidence and the charges were dropped.

One year later, it became known that Judy Johnson suffered from a psychiatric illness. She had in fact accused a number of other people, besides Ray Buckley, of abusing her son. These included her former husband, employees of the Los Angeles health club and a member of the Los Angeles school board. She had told prosecutors that Ray Buckley could fly, and that he and other McMartin preschool workers had put staples in her son's ears and scissors in his eyes (Crewdson, 1988). Three years later she was found dead from alcohol excess.

By the time her mental state was revealed, however, the situation had already escalated into one of the macro-cases of sexual abuse allegations. Large numbers of children had been interviewed by police, their anxious parents, and then workers at the Children's Institute International. Children who denied abuse would be questioned further. More and more children began to tell stories of bizarre and indecent happenings.

By June 1984 staff at the Institute had interviewed nearly sixty-nine of them. It was alleged that the children had been subjected to years of rape, anal, oral and group sex, naked games, sacrifice of animals and babies, cannibalism and making of child pornography. On the basis of these allegations, the owner of the school, sixty-two year old Peggy McMartin Buckey, was arrested in 1983. Her son, Raymond and daughter Peggy Ann Buckey, and four other child care workers were also arrested. They were charged with ritualistic sexual abuse of three hundred and sixty children over a period of five years.

The case attracted international media attention. Exhaustive investigations revealed no evidence to substantiate the charges, apart from the testimony of children who had undergone extensive "disclosure interviews". Analysis of the interview videotapes shows very clearly that the children were systematically manipulated to admit abuse by bribes, threats and tricks, until they told their "yukky secrets" (Coleman, 1989).

A record-breaking trial which cost fifteen million dollars eventually resulted in all defendants acquitted. Proceedings continued over six years. Ray spent over five years in jail, his mother and sister nearly two years while awaiting their trials.

For those who believe they were innocent, this case demonstrates how state intervention practices can damage children and destroy the lives of innocent people. For those who still believe they were guilty, the case represents the way the system can fail to protect abused children and allow offenders to go free. Even books by professional leaders in the sexual abuse field, such as 'Nursery crimes: sexual abuse in daycare' (Finkelhor et al, 1988), cite this case as an example of terrible sexual abuse, totally ignoring the overwhelming evidence that the allegations did not result in convictions of the alleged abusers.

Country Walk Babysitting Service, Florida.

In 1984, stories of widespread satanic abuse of children, especially in nursery schools, were hitting the headlines across America. In particular, the McMartin and Jordan (discussed later in this chapter) cases were attracting huge publicity. Parents were warned of the dangers which might await in even the most innocent-looking day-cares, and advised to check out their children carefully for signs of abuse.

In this climate, in July 1984 several parents came up with some vague concerns about their children, who had been attending the Country Walk Babysitting Service. This was run by a young Latin American woman, Iliana Fuster, in her own home. Her husband, Frank Fuster, ran an interior decorating business, and was occasionally in his office at home during the day. Frank's seven year old son from a previous marriage, Jamie, also lived with them.

There were two incidents which seemed suspicious to parents. The first was a three year old boy who apparently told his mother "Iliana kisses all the babies' bodies", which the mother interpreted to mean that she kissed their genitals. The other was a preverbal nineteen month old boy whose mother thought he looked "glassy-eyed and drugged" on one occasion when she picked him up from the babysitting service. Apart from this, none of the children who had attended Country Walk in the three years it had been running, had been showing any signs of distress. The parents got together, compared stories, and alerted other parents of children being looked after at the Fusters'.

The police were approached, and requested to investigate. They enlisted the assistance of a couple, Laurie and Joseph Braga, psychologists trained in child developmental psychology. The Bragas had been publicly campaigning about how sexual abuse was widespread in America, claiming "one in four females...and one in six males will be molested or raped by the time they are eighteen" (Hollingsworth, 1986). They volunteered their services free of charge.

Children were interviewed by the Bragas. Using anatomical dolls the Bragas named Iliana and Frank, stories of sexual abuse started to emerge. One four year old boy began to talk of bizarre and hideous acts. These included sex games involving smearing of faeces ("ca-ca") on bodies, and eating it. He gave stories of oral sex by Iliana and Frank on all the children, including the babies, of Frank raping little girls, sodomising baby boys, and forcing the children to have sex with each other. He talked about Frank threatening the children with knives and guns, making them watch rituals where birds had their heads cut off, and making videotapes of these activities. He also told of seeing monsters coming out of the toilet, and going for rides on whales and sharks.

The other children denied that anything had happened, but as the interviews progressed, more children began to tell similar stories. Later interviews with the children were videotaped. Examination of these tapes by psychiatrist Lee Coleman revealed the use of leading questions, selective reinforcement of answers about abuse, and modelling with the dolls. The children were encouraged to play "let's pretend" games about what had happened to them, and then their answers were taken to indicate what had really happened. It was believed that children feel safer disclosing if they can describe events as dreams or fantasy. Children were also told what the other children had been claiming had happened.

Frank was arrested and taken into custody in August 1984. The interrogations continued. Three weeks later Iliana was also arrested. Charged with "sexual battery and lewd and lascivious assaults", they both strongly proclaimed their innocence. Examination of the children at a Rape Treatment Centre showed no signs of abuse. A search of the Fuster's house could find none of the alleged props, such as videotapes or camera, masks, or drugs now claimed to have been used on the children. There was nationwide outrage. The case was publicised extensively, and hysterical parents gave media conferences. Some of the children now started to show signs of distress, including nightmares, aggressive and sexually-inappropriate behaviours and other emotional problems.

Both Frank and Iliana continued to deny all allegations through the pretrial hearing in April 1985. It became clear that if found guilty, both would spend the rest of their lives in prison. The trial took place in August 1985. At the last moment, Iliana changed her plea to guilty, claiming that some of the events had taken place but that Frank had made her do it. Frank was found guilty, and sentenced to one hundred and seventy-five years incarceration. Iliana received a ten-year sentence, eligible for parole after five years.

One of the main inconsistencies in the defence case was that apparently examination of Frank's son Jamie diagnosed gonorrhoea of his throat. Gonorrhoea was not detected in any of the other children, nor in either Iliana and Frank. One possibility is that this was a false positive result, which will occur in a small percentage of such tests. As the boy was given treatment as soon as he was diagnosed, there was no chance of repeating the test. Jamie could offer no explanation of how he could have contracted this disease. He repeatedly denied participating in all of the sexual activities alleged by some of the other children. Just before the trial he had several interrogations by the Bragas. In the last of these Jamie was told that he was lying and encouraged to admit that Frank had put his penis in Jamie's mouth. Finally, Jamie agreed it had happened. However, he refused to give evidence at the trial and later recanted, saying that it was not true and he had only said it was under pressure.

The Wee Care Day Nursery, New Jersey.

In April 1985, a four year old boy was having his temperature taken rectally by a nurse. He commented that his preschool teacher did the same thing at nap time. When asked what he meant, he said "her takes my temperature". The teacher was Kelly Michaels, a twenty-three year old actress who had worked as teacher's aide at the Wee Care Centre for seven months, and had recently resigned to take up a job elsewhere. It later transpired that in fact Kelly did take his temperature at preschool, with a plastic strip placed on his forehead.

However, this conversation alerted the boy's mother to the possibility that he was being sexually abused at preschool. He was taken for questioning by the Child Abuse Unit of the county prosecutor's office. The interview was conducted using anatomical dolls, and the boy apparently put his finger in the doll's anus. He also named two other boys who had had their temperatures taken. When these boys were questioned, one claimed Kelly had touched his penis. More and more children were brought in for questioning, and allegations escalated. Parents were called to a meeting run by a social worker who encouraged them to question their children and look for any of the "signs" of abuse. Eventually Kelly was alleged to have sexually abused all of the fifty-one children who attended the daycare during her employment there.

She was accused of daily abuse of the children in her care. This involved licking peanut butter off their genitals, making them drink her urine and eat her faeces, raping and assaulting them with knives, forks, spoons and toys. It was also claimed that she played the piano in the nude every day. She was supposed to have done this unnoticed by her fellow teachers, administrators, parents and other visitors to the school. Moreover, for the entire 150 days she worked there, not one child said a single thing about any of these crimes - because she had forced them to keep it secret.

Kelly was arrested in May 1985. Shaken and bewildered, she protested her innocence. However, she was remanded in custody. In December she was indicted on 235 counts of abuse against thirty-one children. Her trial began in June, 1987. She had already spent two years in prison.

The evidence consisted largely of the children's testimony, shown to the jury on closed-circuit TV. Some of their claims were clearly outrageous and inconsistent. For instance, one child claimed Kelly had made him push a sword into her rectum. Another child vowed that Kelly had once turned her into a mouse for a while. The prosecutor advised the jury at the beginning of the trial that it was not necessary to believe everything the children said. The judge would not allow the children to be cross-examined by defence psychologists, as he believed it would be too traumatic for them. This violated one of the basic principles of justice - that both sides should be heard in the courtroom.

Parents produced charts of "symptoms" of abuse their children were showing, such as bedwetting, nightmares and behaviour problems. These symptoms had only started after their children's "disclosure" of the abuse.

Eileen Treacy, a child abuse "expert", told the jury that the fact that the children initially all denied any abuse was confirmation that it had happened. A succession of "no, no, no" answers was said to prove the "suppression phase" of the abused child. She claimed that she had never seen a more traumatised group of children.

Despite the evidence of defence psychologist Ralph Underwager, who explained how the ongoing interviewing trains children to give the answers expected of them, Kelly was found guilty of 115 counts of sexual abuse against twenty children, aged from three to five. Ironically, the jury found her not guilty of the very charge that had provoked the entire investigation - anally penetrating the little boy whose temperature she had taken.

Kelly was sentenced to forty-seven years in prison. The children and their parents are convinced that they were victims of hideous sexual abuse. They will fight bitterly against her appeal, and have already vowed they will make sure she is denied parole when first eligible, twelve years after sentencing (Rabinowitz, 1990).

Stop press: Kelly's case finally came to appeal this year. Doubts about her guilt and the bizarre nature of the evidence had multiplied. The appeal court found the evidence did not support her conviction, and she was freed in 1993.

Civic Daycare Centre, Christchurch.

A similar child care case has recently surfaced in Christchurch, New Zealand. In September 1992, a 34 year old child care worker with the Civic Daycare Centre, Peter Ellis, was charged with indecently assaulting a child in his care.

Children who had attended the centre in the six years Peter had worked there were located. The children underwent a series of disclosure interviews, at least some of which were videotaped. The charges began to escalate. Peter was now alleged to make children drink his urine and eat his faeces. Accusations include raping a girl, sexually violating others using his finger or a stick, and urinating on their faces. He is alleged to have stuck a needle into one child's anus, making it bleed.

Peter's four co-workers in the daycare, women in their thirties and forties, were all adamant that the abuse could not have happened. Their stand was reported in the media.

In November, these women were also arrested and charged with abuse. The claims now had a flavour of satanic ritual abuse. Accusations were made that children were taken to a private home, made to spend some time in a tunnel under the house, and then forced to stand naked inside a circle of adults, including all five daycare workers. Charges also included involving the children in making child pornography.

Peter now faced forty two counts of indecent assault between December 1986 and February 1992, involving twenty children aged between two and six years.

In March 1993, a High Court judge heard submissions at a pre-trial hearing. The evidence submitted was publicly suppressed, but the judge dismissed all the charges against them. Many of the charges against Peter Ellis were also dropped, but he still faced 25 allegations. Some of the charges were dropped because the parents withdrew them as witnesses, and some were shown to be completely unfounded. In one case a four year old child admitted that the alleged incident did not happen.

The case was heard before a jury in May 1993. Peter Ellis denied all 25 charges. Again, much of the evidence was suppressed, but relied heavily on videotapes of the disclosure interviews of creche children. The jury found him guilty of 16 of the 25 allegations. Throughout the court process, little weight was given to the fact that so many of the allegations were demonstrated to be fabrications. No-one specifically addressed the issue of how this could happen, and the effect this must have on the children and families involved.

Ellis was a flamboyant man who liked to shock adults with sexual talk, which he freely admits. In my view, however, it is highly unlikely that he indulged in the bizarre activities such as making children drink his urine, or inserting objects up boys' penises, for which he was convicted. I await with interest the outcome of his planned appeal.

Satanic ritual abuse

Believers in satanic ritual abuse maintain that there is a worldwide conspiracy of cults practising ritualistic sexual perversions, murder and cannibalism, despite the complete absence of physical evidence to support these claims.

The information on which these allegations are claimed comes from two main sources. Firstly, there is the testimony of children, especially in the daycare cases as described above. Satanic stories also surface in other situations where children are interrogated by the authorities, including custody battles. Secondly, a large number of adults are now claiming satanic abuse in childhood. They maintain they had no memory of the abuse until their memories were "recovered" in therapy. Stories of ritualistic killing and eating of children are not new. Jews were charged by the Greeks of ritual murder and cannibalism of babies, and first-century Christians were similarly charged by the Romans. Later, during the Middle Ages, Jews were accused of kidnapping Christian babies for use in secret religious sacrifices (the so-called `blood libel'). Just prior to the French Revolution, similar stories emerged about French aristocracy kidnapping poor children and bathing in their blood (Richardson et al, 1991).

Tales of children being kidnapped, usually by monsters or witches, who may cook and eat them, is part of our ancient cultural mythology. Most children are exposed to fairy stories such as Hansel and Gretel. Modern horror novels and films also use themes of kidnap and murder for use of body parts or ritualistic sacrifice. Satanic cult stories are constructed from these same basic myths.

Historians maintain that there is no evidence to support the claim that there have ever been satanic cults engaging in conspiracy and bizarre sexual rituals in the past (Underwager and Wakefield, 1991). That such an organised ongoing satanic network could be carrying out such frequent and bizarre acts without leaving any traces is mind-staggering.

The following describes a few of the more well-known cases, but allegations of satanic abuse now number many thousand.

Jordan, Minnesota.

In 1983, Christine Brown accused a rubbish collector, James Rud, of sexually abusing her daughter in the trailer park where she lived. Other children living in the park were questioned, and they alleged that they had also been abused - but by Christine Brown. She was soon arrested and charged with eighteen counts of sexual misconduct.

A sister and brother-in-law (Helen and Tom Brown) who tried to help her get bail, were then arrested by the prosector for child abuse. Local residents met to protest the arrests. Three of them, including a local policeman, Greg Myers, an automobile painter Robert Benz and his wife Lois, were arrested. Not long after this, Myers' wife and a married couple who had driven the Browns home from jail were also arrested and charged with sexual abuse. Under interrogation, the children made allegations of murder, strange dances and costumes, torture and animals being killed. Later stories even included babies murdered and thrown in the river. Eventually, twenty-four adults were accused of running a sex ring abusing their own and other children. Some forty children were eventually implicated. The children were placed in foster care, and at least some of the time were housed together in a hostel where they could compare each other's testimony.

All but one of the children later admitted they had made up the stories under the pressure of the interviews. The one exception who did not admit to lying was a nine year old girl whose stories were so contradictory it was clear her claims were unreliable (Underwager and Wakefield, 1991).

Robert and Lois Benz were acquitted in September 1984. They were the only ones to stand trial. The other cases fell apart, and eventually all but one of the other charges were dropped. An investigation by a special commissioner concluded that none of the cases could be corroborated. Most of the children spent about eighteen months in foster care before being returned to their homes. However, it took over five years (until 1989) before the last couple had their daughter returned to their care.

The only one convicted was James Rud, the original alleged abuser. Rud had two previous convictions for sexual abuse. In exchange for a reduction in charges against him, he had made a 119 page statement testifying against the other defendants, telling of sex parties involving children and adults. When the charges were dropped, he recanted this statement. He did however plead guilty to abusing Christine Brown's daughter, and was sentenced to imprisonment.

Oude Pekela, the Netherlands.
This case originated in 1988 in Oude Pekela, a small Dutch village (Rossen, 1989). A four and a five year old boy were playing together in some bushes. There was some exploratory sex play, and one of them was slightly injured in his anus, probably from one boy trying to push a twig into the other's anus. The injured boy's mother noticed a spot of blood on his underpants and took him to the family doctor.

The doctor suspected rape by a stranger. He called a public meeting in conjunction with the local police, a psychiatrist and the city council, which was attended by three hundred parents. Parents were told that there was a dangerous child molester operating in the area who may have already abused their children. They were instructed on the signs of sexual abuse and told to question their children.

Reports started to trickle in, rapidly increasing to a flood over the next few months. Initially children talked about strangers giving them sweets and taking them for rides in cars. Soon however, reports were streaming in of children being made to eat faeces, drink urine, watch babies being murdered, being involved in bizarre sexual rites and being forced to participate in pornographic sessions.

School teachers, police and social workers interrogated the children in the daytime, parents at night. Hundreds of children, including nearly every preschooler in the village, reported incidents. It was assumed that keeping the sexual abuse secret was permanently damaging for children, so questioning continued with missionary zeal.

Police investigation found no objective evidence of all these confusing and conflicting claims. There was no pornography to be found, medical examinations showed no signs of injuries, no babies had disappeared. There had simply not been the opportunity for many of the incidents to have happened, as the children had never been missing from their homes. The police believed nothing had happened and declared it was mass hysteria.

There was a public outcry. Parents were convinced the allegations were real and accused the government of covering up for criminals. They also enlisted the media in their cause.

After a year of intensive interrogation and abuse counselling, the children started to show signs of distress: bedwetting, fear of strangers, inappropriate sex play and aggressive behaviour. Stories continued to emerge and be elaborated. At last report (Brossen, 1989), the issue was still unresolved, and the interviews and "therapy" have continued.

Orkney Islands.

In February 1990 three children talked about being involved in a circle of dancers in an Orkney quarry. When questioned by a social worker, the children claimed that a hooded figure in the middle would reach in and grab one of the dancers with his crook to be his sexual partner. Two sisters, aged seven and eight, said he had had intercourse with them. The man was said to be the Reverend Morris McKenzie, the parish minister.

The children also named others who were present. Based on allegations of these children, a further nine children were taken from their homes in dawn raids. The police believed a "sex ring" must be operating, and all the children were flown to the Scottish mainland and placed in foster homes.

Nearly two years later, a judicial inquiry headed by Lord Clyde looked into the social workers' actions. Their report released in October 1992 concludes that the police and local authorities acted too quickly and without thinking. Although the inquiry was not to determine the validity of the allegations, Lord Clyde has said that the people at the centre of the affair "should be presumed innocent".

Rochdale, Manchester

In June 1990, a six year old boy was reported by his teachers to be telling stories about black magic and killing babies. When questioned, he implicated a number of other children. Social workers and police abruptly removed seventeen children from their parents into foster care. The children were subjected to weeks of interrogation by child protection workers, and allegations were made that the children had all been victims of a secret satanic cult involving them in sexual rituals.

The media responded with sensational headlines condemning the parents. However, later more-investigative reporting suggested that perhaps the government workers had acted unjustly. A judicial inquiry found the parents innocent and criticised the actions of the police and social workers. The children were returned to their families in March 1991, after nine months separation.

Investigation revealed that in 1988, several Manchester social workers attended training in the United States on how to identify ritual abuse. It was on their return that their interrogation of the Rochdale children "uncovered" satanic abuse. Their preconceptions that satanism and sexual abuse was widespread and that these children were such victims, actually resulted in their priming the children with the accounts they were expecting to hear (Victor, 1991).

Alternative communities

Allegations of sexual abuse of children growing up in intentional communities have been widespread in the last decade. Many of these are in the United States, including Esalen, the New Life Centre, Encounter Inc and the Rajneesh Community. Others include Frederikshof in Germany, the Children of God Communities in Australia and France, and New Zealand's Centrepoint Community.

Most of these groups began in the sexually permissive 1960s and 1970s, and those that have survived have had to make ongoing adjustments to their behaviour in the anti-sexism of the 1980s and 1990s. A group of clinical sexologists at California's Institute for the Advanced Study of Human Sexuality has made an extensive evaluation of sexuality in a large number of intentional communities, and come to the following conclusions (McIlvenna, 1992):

- sexual experimentation was a part of all the intentional communities;
- the experimentation decreased the longer the community was in existence;
- the main criticism by the community at large towards libertinism;
- where families and children were involved in the intentional communities, the children were guided by the sexual standards of the primary community and not the outside community;
- from each community there was an exodus of people who left over disagreements about sexual standards and conduct, and these people often became the leading critics;
- the children growing up in these communities tended to adjust the same as

other children - neither more liberal nor conservative than "townies";
- the most vigorous criticism of the communities came from those who were most threatened by the community's announced intention. For example, a religious community would be criticised by traditional religionists, a therapeutic community by psychologists and psychotherapists.

Persecution of intentional communities, including sexual abuse allegations, tend to follow a common pattern. The initial charges are often made by ex-members of the group, particularly in communities headed by a charismatic leader. It is often those who have been the most devout and ardent followers of the leader's values who become his or her most bitter critic on leaving.

Allegations are reported to police or social services, and full-scale investigations usually ensue. These are often regarding alleged historical events, maybe ten to fifteen years on. In many of these cases, there is some genuine foundation for the allegations. In the early days of sexual experimentation, inappropriate sexual contact will sometimes have occurred between children and adults. This will usually only have surfaced as a problem for the children when they will have been later confronted by the more sexually repressive mores of the community at large, particularly in the anti-sex climate of the late eighties and early nineties. This current climate defines their early experiences as abusive and harmful.

Children of God, Australia.
The Children of God movement was started by David Berg (also known as David Moses) in California in the 1960s. By 1974 there were an estimated six thousand members in seventy countries, including about one thousand in Australia. In its first few years, the movement advocated sexual freedom for its followers. The cult has been accused of promoting sex between adults and children in the 1970s, although the sect denies that this is true.

In May 1992, police and social welfare workers seized over one hundred and thirty children from the Children of God Family in Victoria and New South Wales, Australia. The children were taken from their homes in dawn raids and placed in protective care. The parents were accused of involving the children in bizarre sexual practices and the case made international headlines.

All the parents accused vehemently denied the charges. At least one of the cases involved allegations made against his ex-wife by a father who had left the sect. When the cases were heard in Children's Courts between August and November 1992, it was apparent that the authorities had no evidence to back their allegations. All charges of sexual abuse were dismissed, and the children were returned to their families. The members of the cult concerned are now considering seeking compensation for the abuse they have suffered from social services and police.

Centrepoint Community, Auckland, New Zealand.

Centrepoint Community was started by its spiritual leader, Bert Potter, in 1978. It was a therapeutic community that advocated sexual openness as a path towards spiritual growth. It provided psychotherapeutic services for both its own members and the community at large.

Giving children negative messages about sexuality was believed to be harmful to their emotional growth. Although initiation of sexual contact with children by adults was never condoned, children and adolescents were often not discouraged when they showed an interest in sexual activities. Some parents encouraged their children to be sexually active and praised them for being so. Several teenage girls regularly initiated sexual contact with adult men, and some entered ongoing relationships before the age of consent.

As the Community took shape in its first year, several of the politically effective and prestigious women in the community modelled frequent and public sex with a variety of partners, especially Bert. Some teenagers and younger girls who were concerned with social position and approval found their route clearly mapped out for them. Those of a more independent nature followed their own inclinations to a much greater extent.

This sexual experimentation tended to wane as the community matured, and as public awareness of the sexual abuse of children started to surface in the early 1980s. When I first became associated with the community in 1986 (as described in the foreword), my background in the sexual abuse field lead me to look carefully for signs of child exploitation. I ran a workshop on sexual abuse for community members, wrote about it in their magazine and discussed sexual exploitation with the teenagers, both at a group meeting and individually.

Some of teenagers, both girls and boys, were sexually active under the age of consent, although many were not. This was no different in my experience to teenagers in many other societies in which I had practised medicine. They appeared exceptionally well-informed regarding safe-sex practices. Most of their partners were their peers, and none claimed they were engaging in sexual activities under pressure. Several did however identify a couple of adult community men whom they felt sexually harassed them verbally and visually. These men were spoken to by myself and others about their leering and their sexual innuendos, which appeared to solve the problem.

The teenagers at this time numbered over forty, and acted as a strong peer support group. They also had a voice at the community members' weekly meeting, where they could air any concerns. They had well-developed skills in speaking about intimate matters to a number of adults and acting in assertive ways to get what they wanted. I believed that they were at less risk of rape there than in the wider community.

There were several young people, especially girls, who confided that in the past they had felt under considerable pressure to be sexually active. This pressure was particularly from their peers, especially several young women who had now left the community. They had also felt pressure from their parents, and from the community guru, Bert, with whom I discovered a number had been sexually active in the past.

Many of the founding members had left the Community in the mid-eighties, and some became bitter critics of their ex-spiritual leader and his Community, whose values they no longer followed. Their attitudes and behaviour developed in the direction of the more-sexually conservative, and several had become involved in sexual abuse work.

As the years went by, the acrimony of some of these ex-members grew. Some, although by no means all, had witnessed, encouraged, or even participated in sexual activities with children in the founding years of the Community (1978 to 1982). In line with current social thinking, they now believed that this had seriously and permanently harmed the young people involved. Some felt guilty about their past behaviour, and angry towards the Community, and especially Bert its leader, for allowing and encouraging such things to happen.

Many believed that children living at the community were still under pressure to be sexually active with adults, despite reassurances from myself and some of the senior Community members.

Some ex-members who now worked in the sexual abuse field had contact with many of those who had grown up at Centrepoint and raised with them their possible sexual abuse there. The potential damage from adult-child sexual contact was emphasised, no matter if they thought they were fully consenting and enjoyed it at the time.

Meetings of young people who had spent childhood or adolescent years at Centrepoint were held. The police attended at least one of these meetings, and sought statements from potential complainants. Ongoing sexual abuse counselling was arranged and financial compensation negotiations initiated with the government-run Accident Compensation Commission. Several had over thirty counselling sessions, and some were to receive lump sum payments ranging from about $10,000 to $55,000.

Eventually five young women were to press charges of indecent assault against eleven men and two women. Some of the complainants revealed that they only realised they had been sexually abused from undergoing counselling and from talks amongst themselves and with others. Although they had had a number of sexual partners before the age of consent, the people charged were mostly key members of the Centrepoint Community, especially doctors and therapists, and of course the community leader, Bert Potter.

The arrests were made in a dawn raid on the Community, an operation involving about one hundred and fifty police and other law enforcement officials. It was accompanied by full media coverage, including filming from a helicopter overhead.

Included on the warrant was search and seizure of child pornographic material, as the police claimed they had evidence of Centrepoint involvement in an international "kiddie-porn" network. No such material was recovered, and the arrests could have easily be carried out by telephoning the people concerned and requesting their attendance at the police station.

The incidents were alleged to have occurred between 1978 and 1982. Mostly these were claims of oral sexual contact or genital fondling, sometimes in threesome situations (for example, from Bert Potter and his wife Margie). It was not denied that these experiences had sometimes been initiated by the young women. Had they been accused at the time of the offences, they might have been charged with unlawful carnal knowledge. However, subsequent changes in New Zealand law meant that the only charges now possible were of indecent assault and rape. While there was never any suggestion of force or compulsion, the complainants claimed they had felt emotionally coerced to behave in the ways they had.

Unfortunately, more than a decade had elapsed since these episodes. The complainants' memories were recalled through therapy, group sharing, and thinking and writing about their recollections. They would have been influenced by their current-day attitudes and values, and they were likely to have been under considerable pressure from peers, parents, therapists, police and others to remember details and lay charges.

Under these circumstances, evidence is likely to be distorted and contaminated, even though the complainant would sincerely believe in its validity. A number of charges were in fact dropped before going to court. One defendant was acquitted after his two complainants gave contradictory evidence against him.

The trials took place in 1991 and 1992 amidst a media circus. Some of the accused admitted their actions and pleaded guilty; others defended what they were adamant were false accusations but were found guilty anyway. Others went for expediency and pleaded guilty to what they still privately declare were false allegations in order to get shorter sentences, as it became clear that maintaining one's innocence and insisting on a trial generally resulted in double the sentence. All those charged who still lived at Centrepoint were found guilty and received custodial sentences, ranging from nine months to Bert's sentence of a seven and a half years. None of the four defendants who had left Centrepoint received custodial sentences: they either had their charges dropped, were acquitted, or pleaded guilty and were fined. The only non-Centrepoint resident to receive a prison sentence was my husband, John.

In spite of extensive counselling and financial compensation, several of the complainants are reported to still be emotionally disturbed, angry and distressed, unable to lead happy functional lives. I believe that their early sexualisation and parental encouragement to be sexually active was inappropriate. However it also seems clear that the subsequent counselling and legal intervention they have undergone may have contributed to their seeing themselves as seriously and permanently harmed from their childhood sexual experimentation. I believe the complainants themselves were pawns in this process, and I consider the effects of this secondary victimisation could be at least as damaging as any of their childhood sexual experiences.

Much of the action against Centrepoint, like that experienced by other alternative communities, was fuelled by moral outrage from ex-members, police and social agencies. One judge accused Centrepoint members of ritualistic abuse of children.

Although repeated investigations by the Department of Social Welfare did not uncover any evidence of recent abuse, the Community's critics continued to accuse Centrepoint of sexually abusing its children.

Branch Davidians, Waco, Texas.

Even fundamentalist Christian communities are not immune from these allegations. It was accusations of child sexual abuse that spurred America's Bureau of Alcohol, Tobacco and Firearms and the FBI to storm David Koresh's Branch Davidians sect in Waco, Texas this year (1993). Many cult members and their lawyers have insisted such charges were baseless (*New Zealand Herald*, 5 May 1993). With most of the members now dead, we are unlikely to ever really know what had been going on.

What is clear however, is that the authorities' outraged response to the possibility of Koresh having sex with children lead to their attack on the cult using guns and armoured vehicles. A second assault following a seven week siege ended in a fire which levelled the compound, killing 86 people. Ironically, this tragedy caused the death of about twenty children, whose lives the authorities aimed to protect by their actions.

Cooperite sect, South Island, New Zealand.

In July 1993 the Christian sect called the Cooperites suffered similar allegations when their leader, Neville Cooper, was arrested and charged with indecent assault. He has denied the charges. Founded in the late 1960s, the sect consists of about two hundred people living on two self-sufficient farm properties in the South island of New Zealand.

Based on very strict Christian principles, the cult has always advocated modest dress and forbidden any sexual activity outside of marriage. They have always emphasised the importance of a happy active sex life within wedlock, however. Members often marry at a young age and both men and women are taught that they must satisfy their partners sexually.

In a familiar pattern, the allegations against Neville Cooper are a result of complaints from disillusioned ex-members of his community. We await the outcome of his prosecution.

Child pornography

Child pornography began to be perceived as a serious problem in the Western world about the mid-1970s. In the United States, a crusade against this moral outrage rapidly swept the country. Feminist organisations, religious groups, politicians, police and the media continue to campaign relentlessly about the scourge of child pornography.

Few people would condone the production of material which sexually demeans, exploits or assaults children. However, the emotional hysteria which surrounds the topic clouds a rational appraisal of the quantity and content of the material that is actually available.

In 1976 a journalist named Robin Lloyd published a book entitled 'For Money or Love: Boy Prostitution in America', in which he claimed the existence of a huge prostitution network involving 300,000 boys. In fact, the figure of 300,000 was merely a working hypothesis of Lloyd's, with no empirical basis. However, it was taken to be a reliable statistic by Judianne Densen-Gerber, director of the Odyssey House chain of treatment clinics for drug addicts.

Denser-Gerber multiplied the figure by two, as she believed 300,000 girls would also be involved in such activities. Since Loyd had claimed that the real figure would be twice what he could statistically validate, she then multiplied it by two again, reaching an estimate of over one million children involved in sex for money. She presented these figures to a House of Representatives hearing for a first Federal law against child pornography. The chairman of the hearing, John Conyers, doubled the number again because he reasoned that America had not only one million runaways, but also one million school drop outs. He concluded that there were over two million children in his country being sexually exploited by prostitution and pornography (Schuijer and Rossen, 1992). The law was passed unanimously.

The media took up the cause and newspapers and television were flooded with stories about the evils of child pornography. The FBI, US Postal Service and US Customs cooperated in an extensive three-year investigation, and published their report in 1980. They found the claims that minors were involved in pornography were grossly exaggerated, and in fact the police and justice officials had been unable to find any evidence of production of child pornography on a commercial scale. The FBI carried out nationwide raids on sixty pornographic distributors throughout the country, but were unable to find any child pornography. The report demonstrated the unsubstantiated basis on which the original figures had been made.

However, the figures of Lloyd and Densen-Gerber were accepted as fact by the media and official agencies, who continue to make extravagant claims about a multibillion dollar child pornography industry (Rush, 1980; Schuijer and Rossen, 1992).

Anti-pornography laws were being dismantled in Scandinavia around 1970, and there was some commercial production of child-porn magazines and films in Sweden and Denmark, and also in Holland and West Germany, in the late 1960s through to the 1970s. Some of this material did find its way into the United States. Relatively few child pornography magazines were actually printed in the United States.

There has never been any evidence of the rumoured "snuff" films, and no children featuring in pornographic material have ever been known or even suspected of being victims of murder (Stanley, 1989; Schuijer and Rossen, 1992). A study by researchers Schuijer and Rossen revealed that no snuff movies had ever been discovered anywhere in the world, nor reported in any criminological or sexological literature they could find. They concluded that snuff movies do not in fact exist.

In the early 1980s, countries which had liberalised pornography laws began to reverse their decisions. Denmark and Sweden prohibited the commercial distribution of child pornography, followed by the Netherlands in 1987.

By the end of the 1980s, there was no evidence of child pornography being produced commercially in either Europe or the States, and what material was found was being made by amateurs for private use or sale to friends and acquaintances (Stanley, 1989).

Despite low numbers of convictions for child pornography offences, American government agencies have been operating extensive entrapment operations. Their methods include creating phoney organisations, newsletters and advertisements offering to sell child pornography. Their advertisements are often merely suggestive or ambiguous. Some operations have involved the production of actual material describing sexual fantasies with children and even photographs of children playing and posing nude.

"Target lists" have been compiled by law enforcement agencies. These names come from a number of sources, including individuals who have been the intended customers of adult pornography seized by United states Customs. The American Postal Service and Customs have marketed and sold child pornography videotapes and magazines to individuals, who were subsequently arrested. Most of the child pornography arrests from 1984 to 1986 were the result of these sting operations, and some of the unsuspecting buyers may not have known what they were buying, or would not have bought child pornography if it had not been offered to them (Schuijer and Rossen, 1992).

More recently, there has been a marked increase in prosecutions for possession of child pornography, especially photographs. What actually constitutes child pornography is not clear-cut. The American first child pornography law of 1977 stipulates that images of nudity are prohibited, if they are 'depicted for the purpose of sexual stimulation or gratification of any individual who may see such depiction'.

In the prevailing climate in America, the definition has been increasingly broadened, and is now often interpreted to include any photograph of a naked child. The prohibition may include all pictures revealing naked genitals of any minor (under eighteen years old), and the breast area of any girl who is less than eighteen years.

In some cases, parents have been prosecuted for taking photographs of their own children nude, and even for 'naked on the fur rug' pictures of their babies (Stanley, 1989). Parents who have innocently photographed naked children playing, sunbathing, or in the bath, have unwittingly handed in rolls of film to local film processors and found themselves arrested and their children removed by child protection workers. Last year a patient of mine told me how her husband had been arrested and charged with producing child pornography after photographing his daughters doing yoga exercises in the nude and then handing the film into a local store for processing.

Non-exploitative child nudity is being increasingly censored in the United States. Nudist magazines no longer contain photographs of children. Sex education books which show children's bodies have been withdrawn from distribution. Pictures of nude children have disappeared from legitimate art photography books. Such an extreme stance has not occurred in Europe, where such material is still freely available.

Alarmist stories of child pornography continue. In New Zealand in 1992 the media reported the existence of a list of names of an international paedophile network uncovered by the FBI and the Australian police. These people were claimed to be actively seeking child porn videos and four thousand New Zealanders, including several prominent names, were alleged to be included on the list (*Sunday News*, 2nd August 1992). Horrified citizens called for publication of the list in the newspapers. Police investigation found the names had no proven link to child pornography, and the list was not circulated.

As mentioned above, police claimed that the New Zealand Centrepoint Community were involved in manufacture and international distribution of child pornography, despite no evidence to substantiate their accusation. The media continued to imply that the Community has been active in this way (*NZ Herald*, 1st October 1992).

Child pornography certainly has and still does exist. It was produced and sold in Europe and the States in the 1970s. The Protection of Children from Sexual Exploitation Act of 1977 quickly put a stop to virtually all the child exploitation from pornography in America, and revised laws in Europe largely halted creation of such material there.

Child pornography sexually exploits children and is not to be condoned. However, propaganda about the extent and nature of the problem has been disseminated by 'misinformation, deception, and intentional distortion of fact' (Stanley, 1989). The ensuing moral panic has resulted in greater state intervention into private lives, and censorship of sex education materials and artistic expression. It has consumed considerable resources without significantly contributing to the very real problems of child abuse and exploitation.

The child pornography myth can be seen to be yet another example of a belief by concerned agencies and individuals that children are being exploited. Emotional overreaction, fuelled by media involvement, then results in the proliferation and dissemination of this misinformation, despite lack of empirical support for the claims.

8. False Complaints

"Heav'n has no rage, like love to hatred turn'd,
Nor Hell a fury, like a woman scorn'd"
William Congreve, 1697.

False allegations of sexual misconduct are not new. The Old Testament (Genesis, 39, 7-20) tells the story of when the Jew, Joseph, is slave to an Egyptian named Potiphar. His master's wife, Zuleika, is attracted to Joseph and asks him to lie with her, but he always refuses. One day Joseph goes to their house to do some business and he and Zuleika are alone. When he again refuses her advances, she takes hold of his clothes. However, he pulls away, leaving his clothes in her hands, and flees. When the other men arrive, she claims that Joseph "*came in unto me to lie with me, and I cried out in a loud voice: and it came to pass, when he heard that I lifted up my voice and cried, that he left his garment with me and fled, and got him out*". She repeats this story to her husband on his return. Potiphar's "wrath was kindled" and he had Joseph put into prison.

This is a clear case of a malicious act of retribution by a scorned woman. As already discussed, false allegations of sexual abuse range from the deliberate to the unintentional. Many false accusations are not in fact conscious lies, but the result of misunderstanding about the nature of recalled memories. False memories can be inadvertently created through processes of investigation or therapy. In such cases, false complaints may be laid by people who sincerely believe they are genuine.

There are also several other causes and motives for false allegations of sexual abuse. Again, these range from the inadvertent to the deliberate. This chapter discusses the more common of these, although the list is by no means exhaustive.

One of the areas where there is a large percentage of false abuse claims is in access and custody battles when parents separate or divorce. This may result from being overly suspicious of a now-distrusted spouse, or may be a deliberate ploy to hurt and get revenge.

Less commonly, teenagers have been known to make false allegations against their parents and other adults as acts of retribution. False accusations may also arise from pressure to lay complaints from peers, parents and people in authority.

Increasingly there are payoffs in defining oneself as a victim in modern society. A history of sexual abuse can be blamed for all one's emotional and social problems as an adult. In some parts of the world, especially Hollywood, it has even become a fashionable thing to claim. There may also be financial gains for both the victim and her (less frequently his) therapist.

Custody cases

Custody cases are one area where there is a relatively large percentage of false allegations. These cases include retaliation against an ex-spouse in custody battles, or angry feelings towards an ex-lover when the relationship has soured. Such action may be deliberately encouraged by unscrupulous lawyers, who know how effective it can be. There again, the false complaint may not be created at a conscious level and memories of what happened may be reframed in the light of current feelings toward the alleged offender, or through therapy.

False allegations during divorce and custody dispute have been increasingly recognised and studied (Bresee et al, 1986; MacFarlane, 1986; Paradise et al, 1987; Jones and McGraw, 1987; Ross and Blush, 1990; Wakefield and Underwager, 1990; Blush and Ross, 1990; Sheridan, 1990; Wakefield and Underwager, 1991; Herman, 1992). These cases have become a serious problem for professionals, who must determine whether the abuse is real in a particular case.

There is much to be gained by making false allegations of sexual abuse in child access or custody battles between parents. If the allegations are upheld, the accusing parent wins custody of the child, and the other parent is denied any contact. The avenging parent causes the hated former spouse to be severely punished, and receives social approval for doing so. Support and encouragement may be offered by family, friends and social workers. Often the accusing parent's legal costs are borne by the state, but the defending parent can be rendered bankrupt by the proceedings (Wakefield and Underwager, 1991).

Deliberately fabricated allegations are sometimes made by angry, vindictive parents. More commonly, however, a parent becomes hypersensitive to the possibility of abuse from the ongoing exposure to the topic from the media, child protection programmes and the wide-spread publication of the so-called behavioural indicators. Children who have recently experienced a hostile separation or divorce of their parents are likely to be showing signs of stress and will probably be exhibiting some of these behavioural signs. A bitter and worried parent may make a premature assumption that the ex-partner has been abusing their child. Suggestive questioning can then shape the expected responses, and involvement of sexual abuse validators will unknowingly continue this process.

Most studies show that abuse is substantiated in custody cases only 50% of the time at best (Jones and McGraw, 1987; Wakefield and Underwager, 1990). However, as explained before, figures are generally hard to interpret. What must be asked in particular is what constitutes substantiation in each study. What is often measured is not whether or not abuse has occurred, but the opinions of the people involved and what the justice system has decided happened. The true incidence of abuse may be substantially less than some papers suggest.

I have examined court and interview transcripts of a number of New Zealand custody cases involving sexual abuse allegations, where there is clearly evidence that the accusations are false.

A representative sample of these is a case involving four year old twins, whom I shall call Cathy and Paul. Their mother Bronwyn had been trying to prevent the children's father Terry from having access to them for several months. In fact, since their separation Terry had only had contact with his children during the daytime on Saturdays, and always in the company either of his parents or latterly his new girlfriend Eve.

The twins had been difficult children from an early age. Cathy tended to be clingy and Paul was prone to tantrums. These problems continued or even worsened following their parents' separation, and the children were referred to a Child and Family Guidance Centre. On examining the Centre's notes, it is clear that right at the beginning there was an obvious assumption by the therapists involved that the children's behaviour problems were due to sexual abuse. At the beginning of the very first assessment session, the children were asked if their father ever cuddled or touched them in ways they did not like (their answer is no). Their mother claimed both children had complained of sore genitals after their access visits.

The children then underwent intensive sexual abuse interrogations. Cathy's interview lasted one and a quarter hours. The interviewer, Sarah, introduced anatomical dolls at the onset, which she suggested were Cathy, Paul, Bronwyn and Terry. She introduced the idea of loving touch and hurting touch and suggested that daddy had done some naughty touching. Cathy's repeated denials were completely ignored by Sarah, who returned again and again to the topic.

S: Did daddy ever put his diddle near your vagina?
C: (laughing) No.
S: Can you show me how he did that.
C: But my dad didn't do it.
S: Your dad didn't? Who did?
C: Nobody...

S: Did any other dad want to do that?
C: No.

Cathy got obviously puzzled and bored by the conversation and tried to change the subject and talk about the toys in the playroom. Sarah was relentless, however, in pursuing the topic of sore vaginas and naughty touching.

S: Cathy, when you go and see dad, I wonder if dad sometimes makes your vagina sore.
C: No he doesn't.
S: If he did it would be okay to tell me.
C: He doesn't.
S: But mummy said that you had a sore vagina.
C: Yeah, I used to.
S: We want to help so you don't get any more sore vaginas.
C: I used to have one, but now it's gone. I used to have one at home at mums.

Cathy never agreed that daddy had done naughty things to her, but finally Sarah called her mother into the room and got Bronwyn to ask her if daddy had ever touched her vagina. Cathy was encouraged by the two adults to tell, to be a "good brave girl" and finally she said yes.

C: Yep ... he squeezes it, he squeezed everything on my body. He squeezed my fingers. He squeezed everything.
S: Well he was a very naughty daddy wasn't he to do that?
C: Will the policeman put him in jail for that?
S: How did you know that dads sometimes go to jail if they do that?
C: Because mum told me. Didn't you mummy?

Paul was also shown the dolls at the beginning of the interview, and helped to undress them. He claimed the only naughty thing his daddy had ever done to him was to smack him. Sarah kept encouraging him, asking him to show her with his hands on the doll what daddy did. Eventually Paul came to say that the daddy doll touched the boy doll all over. The transcript continued:

P: He pulled everything.
S: He pulled everything.
P: He pulled my hair and...
S: Did it hurt Paul's penis? Did it make it sore?
P: Yeah.

Paul was encouraged to hit the daddy doll "as hard as you want". With Sarah's clear approval, he threw the doll around and later bit it all over, including its penis. Sarah interpreted this to mean that Paul had been made to have his father's penis in his mouth, even though Paul denied this when asked. Paul repeatedly contradicted his story, and when asked again about his daddy "pulling his penis", claimed adamantly that it never happened.

At the conclusion of these sessions, Sarah was sure that both children had been severely and repeatedly sexually abused by their father. The police were notified and Terry was arrested and charged. After a week in jail, he was released on bail.

The children had a number of further assessment interviews, and were questioned extensively by their mother. On one occasion during breakfast, Paul described a dream he had about Terry's girlfriend Eve being dressed as a witch. He and Cathy then elaborated and the story changed from a dream to something believed to have actually happened.

The witch costume was described in detail, and in fact is later recognised by Eve and Terry to be that of Bad Jelly the Witch, whom the children had watched on television during one of their visits. Eve was said to have chased them, and put her fingers up their anuses and in Cathy's vagina. The stories got progressively more bizarre, with incidents such as Terry having put his whole hand, covered by a blue rubber glove, inside Cathy's vagina (a medical examination revealed an intact hymen).

As the interrogations continued, the twins started to show more and more disturbed behaviour, with nightmares, fear of witches, and unsettled behaviour at school. They became terrified they might see their father driving in a car and got scared of leaving the house. Once the assessment interviews were over, they were referred for abuse counselling.

The charges against Terry were heard before the High Court. The evidence presented was highly inconsistent and improbable. The jury found there was no evidence of abuse and Terry was acquitted. However, shortly afterwards the local newspaper ran a story about the case, with changed names but clearly identifiable characteristics of Terry and Eve, claiming that they had performed acts of satanic sexual abuse on the children, despite the acquittal.

Terry and his parents were subjected to anonymous phone calls, abusive letters and graffiti ("Terry is a child rapist") painted on their corner store, where Terry worked with them. Eventually his parents were forced to sell their business.

There followed a Family Court hearing to determine custody and access rights. Despite the finding of the High Court, the judge believed that the evidence presented by the psychotherapist who had conducted the interviews and her supervisor proved that Terry had sexually abused the children. He awarded full custody to Bronwyn, and Terry was denied all access.

The sexual abuse counselling continued, and the twins' behaviour continued to deteriorate. They became very disruptive at school, and Paul began to sexually "act out" with Cathy. By the time they were seven, their mother could no longer cope with them and they were placed in a foster home.

This case illustrates many of the typical features of custody cases involving false allegations. There had been an acrimonious separation, with the wife wanting to prevent her ex-husband from seeing the children. The children were showing signs of stress by their worsening behaviour, and clearly the mother had suspected sexual abuse, and already primed the children, before they were seen at the Guidance Centre.

The interviewer was operating from the assumption that these children had definitely been abused by their father, and used cueing, modelling with anatomical dolls and selective reinforcement to obtain the evidence she expected to hear. No amount of denial or inconsistencies, or even stories that were obviously fantasy, would sway her belief.

Teaching children that their stories and fantasies actually happened can leave them very confused about the nature of reality. Evidence indicates that this can leave a child mentally disturbed or even psychotic (Underwager, 1986). They will probably come to believe that the terrible things did actually happen to them. Months or years of abuse therapy trains children that they are victims, and often leaves them afraid of the alleged offender and of the world in general, which they see as a place where adults are likely to hurt children. Months of dealing with bizarre and violent sexual acts may distort children's development towards healthy adult sexuality. They learn that acting out such behaviours wins adult attention, and these children often show signs of disturbed sexual play.

Cathy and Paul's worsening behaviour after the interrogation and therapy processes is typical of the behavioural disturbances frequently seen in such cases (Wakefield and Underwager, 1988). Many agencies recognise that this happens.

The brochure from START, a Sexual Abuse Therapy Centre in Christchurch, New Zealand, warns parents to expect a deterioration in their child's behaviour but urges them to continue therapy even if their child appears to be getting worse. They explain this process as "therapy getting all the pain, bad memories, worries, fears and feelings out into the open" although there is no empirical evidence for such a theory. The possibility that such behaviour might also be due to the confusion and conflict caused by reinventing a child's history, is not addressed.

The world's most publicly fought custody case is the battle over Hilary Morgan. This has been the subject of talk shows, magazine stories and television documentaries as well as news reports. Hilary was born in the United States, the daughter of Dr Elizabeth Morgan, a plastic surgeon, and Dr Eric Foretich, an oral surgeon. After a bitter separation, Dr Morgan accused Dr Foretich of sexually abusing their daughter, which he repeatedly denied. The courts found no evidence of abuse.

However, to prevent his access to his daughter, Hilary's mother hid her away and spent over two years in prison rather than reveal the whereabouts of the little girl. Her father spent years searching for her and eventually she was found in Christchurch, New Zealand, living with her maternal grandparents.

Dr Morgan moved to New Zealand on her release from jail and a Christchurch Family Court judge granted her sole custody of Hilary, with the condition that she refrained from publicising the case in New Zealand. Should she ever return to the United States, she would have to face a contempt charge. Moreover, a warrant for Hilary's seizure is still active there and in two hundred other countries. New Zealand laws are unusual in not upholding this warrant. As a result, Christchurch has become the centre of activity in an underground network which assists parents, especially from America, in hiding children from ex-partners wanting access.

Dr Foretich travelled to Christchurch to meet with Hilary, who is now ten years old and does not know the father from whom she has been separated since she was a tiny child. It is likely that she believes he did abuse her; apparently the reunion was an awkward one, and her father is not contesting the custody ruling, as long as Hilary is not subjected to any further publicity.

Teenage retribution

Although far less common, there are an increasing number of cases recorded of teenagers deliberately making false allegations against adults they believe have been unfair or cruel to them, to get revenge.

Most commonly these are of teenagers making false claims of abuse against their parents or foster-families. These have sometimes been acts of retribution for unpopular rules and disciplinary measures which the teenager has considered unjust.

In 1985 an Australian medical practitioner, Dr Dennis Johnston (pseudonym), suffered false allegations of sexual molestation from his thirteen year old stepdaughter, who was angry about issues such as the hours she could stay out at night and the number of dances she was allowed to attend. The case was shown to be clearly fabricated and he was never charged, but Dr Johnson experienced harrowing interviews from the police and his wife suffered suspension of her licence as a daycare worker because she supported him (Wilson, 1986).

Everson and Boat (1989) describe a number of cases where adolescents have made allegations for revenge, to escape punishment, or for other gain. In one case, a twelve year old girl accused her mother's new boyfriend of having touched her inappropriately. She later admitted that her step-father had paid her $5 to make the claim. Another thirteen year old girl explained that her false allegation against her father was because she resented having to go to church with her parents and wanted more freedom.

Everson and Boat also describe a number of cases where the allegations are so highly improbable or impossible that they are clearly fabricated. One girl, for example, accused seven different men, including her father, of raping her over the previous two years. Some of the men could prove they were nowhere near the girl during the time of the alleged crimes. Another thirteen year old mildly retarded girl made allegations against numerous family members and acquaintances that were obviously fantasy.

Medlicott (1979) describes several cases of false allegations made by teenagers suffering from schizophrenic illness, where the allegations were shown to be delusional although the stories were described in great detail. Jones and McGraw (1985) also report that a study performed at the Kempe Center found that emotionally disturbed adolescent girls frequently made fictitious allegations.

Malicious complaints have also been made by teenagers against other adults in authority, especially teachers. Following a much publicised trial of a British politician accused of a homosexual liaison, a school teacher was prosecuted in England for behaving immorally with some of his pupils. At the last moment, one of the boys making the complaint confessed that they had made the story up to get revenge on a hated teacher, having got the idea from reading about the politician's trial (Wilson, 1986). In Australia, a school teacher has successfully sued a teenage girl pupil who falsely claimed that he sexually harassed her.

With increasing media coverage of sexual abuse and the proliferation of sexual abuse education programmes in schools, these sorts of accusations are likely to get more and more common.

Pressure from peers, parents, and people in authority

Some false allegation cases have resulted from pressure from other people to disclose abuse. A child or teenager may tell a highly embellished or even fabricated story, which comes to the attention of a parent or an adult in authority. It becomes extremely difficult for the complainant to back down, and the process escalates out of his or her control. Likewise, children and adolescents may come under peer group pressure to claim abuse.

Within the current social climate, circumstances sometimes arise where there is an inverted social status in being a sexual abuse victim. Children who "tell" about abuse may become the centre of attention, be rewarded with praise, cuddles, or sweets and other treats, and sometimes even become celebrities. In some of the cases involving many alleged offenders and victims, such as some of the nursery-school cases (see Chapter 9), children come under considerable pressure from their peers, their parents and the investigating adults, to "jump on the band-wagon". They may experience accusations of being cowardly if they continue to deny that anything happened. Where multiple abuse of children has been suspected, such as in daycare cases, there have been many reported cases of children being told that the other children have already admitted that they have been abused, even though this is not true (Underwager and Wakefield, 1990). It would take an exceptional child to resist such combined forces.

The allegations of sexual abuse at the Centrepoint Community, as discussed in the previous chapter, illustrate clearly the pressures some people come under to define themselves as victims.

I have a statement from a young woman who attended a meeting of some of the complainants, at which a senior police officer was also present. She describes a discussion at the meeting about how victims could claim government compensation: the more serious the abuse, the greater the amount. She writes "*The discussion then started to get very bitter and someone said 'Yeah, we're going to get them' and 'we're gonna make them pay' and things like that. It was quite scary.*"

The police officer asked all those present to make individual statements to him, so that the offenders could be prosecuted. She writes that he told them that "*if we made a statement we wouldn't have to stand up in court if we didn't want to*". She said that she had no statement to make, but he gave her his card and told her to ring him. When she failed to telephone him, he rang her a few days later, again trying to get her to make a statement. She replied that she had no reason to make a statement against anyone.

One of the complainants was still at school, and she received considerable police pressure to lay charges. The police officer in charge of the case made repeated visits to the young woman's home to persuade her to make and sign statements, and even met her at school when her father began to object to the harassment.

Emotional payoff in being a victim

Within the prevailing ideology of victimology, there are sometimes considerable payoffs to be obtained from seeing oneself as a victim. In many educational and vocational areas, there is a general policy of positive discrimination for groups and individuals perceived as being oppressed, and this belief system permeates social thinking with regard to the advantages of being a victim. In some agencies, a 'victim/survivor' of sexual abuse is considered an ideal candidate for employment as a sexual abuse counsellor.

Furthermore, being a victim of sexual abuse can be an excellent scapegoat. Many people who discover that they were abused as children then blame all their social and psychological problems on this experience. This can effectively absolve them from responsibility for their subsequent behaviour.

Ten to twenty years ago, most people would have found admitting that they had been sexually abused a shameful confession. Today, in some circles it is even chic to be a victim. Especially in the United States, there is a stream of national celebrities telling their stories of sexual abuse on talk-shows, docudramas, and in books and magazines.

Oprah Winfrey sobbingly revealed to the world how she was abused by her uncle, a cousin and a family friend. Roseanne Arnold told in graphic detail of vile and bizarre molestations of her and her sisters, which she only remembered when she underwent therapy as an adult. These were supposed to have happened to her from age one to two years (memory studies show that people are very unlikely to have any recall from this age), and her parents and sisters deny the stories.

LaToya Jackson published an autobiography claiming she was a victim of sex and violence as a child and appeared on numerous talk-shows accusing her parents of incest. Princess Elizabeth of Yugoslavia denies that her actress daughter Catherine Oxenberg was mólested as a child, despite Catherine's sensational public claims. Princess Elizabeth believes that the idea was caused by an unscrupulous psychiatrist in Hollywood where "sexual abuse is very fashionable at the moment" (Grutzner, 1992). Many other celebrities have followed this trend.

As well as getting great publicity, these self-confessed victims gain support and sympathy, praise for their honesty and bravery, and may make money out of the situation as well.

Financial gains

For some there is also a financial gain to be made in being a sexual abuse victim. The stars and celebrities mentioned above may make money from their increased publicity, selling their stories to magazines and other media, writing books or making talk-show tours.

For others, a further motive is financial compensation for the trauma suffered from the alleged abuse. In the United States, adults who come to believe through therapy that they were abused as children, seek and often win compensation from the alleged offenders (often their fathers). This may up to hundreds of thousands of dollars.

New Zealand has a government-operated scheme called the Accident Compensation Corporation (now known as the Accident Rehabilitation and Compensation Insurance Corporation), which until recently has been awarding lump sum payments to sexual abuse victims of up to $27,000 per claim. The money is in compensation for "loss of enjoyment of life" as a result of the trauma suffered. The awards are made only when the condition is unlikely to improve. This means that someone making a claim must believe him or herself to be permanently damaged and incurable. Where harm is believed to have been caused by several different events, separate claims are sometimes lodged, each eligible for a lump sum The more severe the impairment is assessed to have been, the greater the payment is likely to be. This could be a powerful incentive for distorting, exaggerating or even fabricating abuse.

Claims with ACC for such payments soared in the early 1990s. 1993 has seen the abolition of lump-sum payments, to be replaced by a weekly allowance subject to review. However, about 100,000 claims were lodged before the cutoff date, which could cost ACC $300 million over two years (*New Zealand Herald*, 3 June 1993).

There is also a financial gain and career advancement for the numerous therapists who have taken up sexual abuse counselling in the last decade. Past sexual abuse is believed to require intensive long-term counselling, often at weekly intervals. In the United States, there are an increasing number of cases where clients with recovered memories of abuse are successfully suing their alleged offenders for counselling costs, as well as compensation payments.

In New Zealand, the cost of sexual abuse counselling is mostly met by the Accident Compensation Corporation who pay ACC-registered counsellors a generous rate of $56 to $78 per hour. In the past, registration criteria have not been strenuous, and have largely consisted of some form of past counselling or social work experience, attendance at a short sexual abuse workers' course, and having read the appropriate literature (usually the book "Courage to Heal", discussed in Chapter 4). Formal qualifications were not required, although criteria are now becoming much more stringent.

In 1992 it was reported that the ACC was spending ten million dollars a year on sexual abuse counselling. This is an extraordinary sum of money for a country with a population of less than four million people. With the reported incidence of abuse still rapidly escalating, the cost to the country for therapy can only continue to rise.

The *New Zealand Herald* (2 December 1992) reported that sexual abuse victims were applying for financial help from the Accident Compensation Corporation at a rate of five hundred a week. About 6000 claims were lodged with the corporation in the three months to September. This was a massive increase compared to a total of 2173 claims in the year to June 1991 and 1075 claims in the preceding twelve months.

To make a claim, all that is required is that the alleged victim and her therapist believe she was abused. The complainant must produce a certificate from a doctor stating she alleges abuse. There is no requirement to substantiate that the abuse occurred and corroborating evidence is not called for. Payment is irrespective of whether any legal charges are made. The *New Zealand Herald* reported that ACC accepted 98% of claims that were laid.

Clients attending a private psychotherapist for emotional problems generally have to pay the fees themselves. If the therapist discovers that in fact their clients have a past history of sexual abuse, their fees may well be met through litigation, from insurance or by the state. There is therefore a huge incentive for therapists to discover abuse and attribute their clients' life problems to that experience. Sexual abuse work has become a gravy-train that many counsellors are (sometimes inadvertently) boarding.

9. The Industry's Contribution to the Sexual Abuse Epidemic

> *"It were better that a hundred witches go free than one innocent person be condemned"*
> Increase Mather, President of Harvard College, 1692, in 'A Case of Conscience'.

> *"I would rather see ten fathers wrongly accused than one child sent back into what could be an abusive situation"*
> Court psychologist, Auckland, 1989.

Western societies are investing ever-increasing sums of money and resources in the battle against child sexual abuse. Despite these attempts, the problem appears to be growing steadily worse. It is painful for the growing body of workers in the sexual abuse industry to consider the possibility that their efforts sometimes contribute to the problem. Good people are engaging in behaviours they genuinely believe are in the best interests of children, yet sometimes the outcomes are disastrous.

Although many authors claim that false allegations are rare (Rush, 1980; Summit, 1983; MacFarlane, 1986), extensive studies by researchers such as Besharov (1985), the former director of the U S National Centre on Child Abuse and Neglect, has indicated that about 65% of suspected child abuse cases are unfounded. The incidence of false reports has increased markedly where mandatory reporting has been introduced. Anonymous telephone hot-lines are similarly exacerbating the problem.

Where sexual abuse therapists and counsellors are motivated by political or religious convictions this may also contribute to heightened suspicion and subsequent detection of abuse.

Where sexual abuse therapists and counsellors believe that if a child denies abuse, contradicts himself/herself, or withdraws previous accusations, then he/she is providing definite proof that abuse has taken place (this is known in these circles as the Child Sexual Abuse Accommodation Syndrome), the incidence of false accusations has also increased markedly.

When sexual abuse therapists and counsellors believe that victims of sexual and satanic abuse dissociate from the experience and forget the events, therapists become committed to unblocking memories of the abuse despite their client's denials that it happened.

When clients describe incidents under hypnosis which they continue to deny are real, the diagnosis of multiple personality disorder is increasingly made.

When child care workers are committed to believing and validating abuse whenever it is suspected, parents and other care givers can sometimes misuse this commitment by fabricating stories of abuse, to obtain the attention and support of the helpers. People who behave in this way suffer from the psychiatric condition Munchausen syndrome by proxy, and more and more of such cases are now being reported.

Medical findings supporting or proving abuse are not as clear-cut as may be expected. Other false allegations have resulted from the use of faulty medical indicators in diagnosing possible abuse.

What is seldom acknowledged by sexual abuse workers is the potentially devastating effects of false allegations on both the children and their families. Many individuals and agencies believe, like the court-appointed psychologist quoted above, that it is better to err on the side of falsely accusing - and frequently convicting - some men, rather than allow possible abuse to continue. They appear not to recognise the damage to children done by this process. Moreover, the flood of reports most agencies now experience over-loads their limited resources and children in real danger are unable to be adequately identified and protected.

Mandatory reporting

In many countries, especially the United States, many professionals and agencies are required by law to report all cases of suspected sexual abuse. Mandatory reporting has been introduced with the best of intentions, to protect children and prevent abuse continuing, but the outcome of this ruling has serious negative repercussions.

In some states in America, health professionals, teachers, social workers, child care workers and police face legal penalties if they fail to report suspected cases. Some laws also make it mandatory for relatives, neighbours, friends of the family, and in some states even complete strangers to report all suspected abuse (Besharov, 1985).

Suspicion of abuse might be merely an observation by a family friend or neighbour that a child is exhibiting signs of stress. Interpreting this as a 'behavioural indicator' may result in a premature assumption that the child has been sexually abused. It may even be a malicious rumour spread by someone with a vested interest in harming the accused. Most mandatory reporting laws maintain the anonymity of the reporters, who will therefore not be held accountable for their information (Howitt, 1992).

Once a suspicion has been reported to the authorities, the case must be investigated. As has already been explained, this process can be self-fulfilling, especially if the investigators believe that abuse has occurred. Mandatory reporting must inevitably increase the percentage of false positives. Unfounded cases of reported child abuse went from 35% in 1975 to 65% ten years later (Besharov), and have continued increase in number since the introduction of obligatory reporting of any suspected abuse. Even if the abuse is later shown to be unfounded, introduction of this law means more and more families experiencing the trauma of the investigation process. Children are usually separated from the accused parent whilst allegations are investigated, and it may be months or even years before the charges are found to be unsubstantiated.

Even a not guilty verdict in a subsequent court case may not restore normal access or relationships. Family courts in New Zealand are able to ignore these verdicts if they believe on less rigorous "expert evidence" that the child may still be in danger.

Introduction of mandatory reporting leads to a deluge of cases to be investigated. The motivation of the reporters might well be their own legal protection rather than what is in the best interest of the child and family concerned.

This flood of cases overloads the limited resources of the social agencies, and genuine cases of abuse are less likely to receive the help and attention they need.

Mandatory reporting laws could erode trust between families and professional workers. Parents might become fearful of community agencies and health professionals and reluctant to ask their advice.

In New Zealand in 1988 the Minister of Social Welfare, Michael Cullen, came under considerable pressure from lobbyists to introduce mandatory reporting legislation in New Zealand. He clearly identified some of the pitfalls in this action, saying that officials in New South Wales had experienced such problems when reporting was enforced and advised New Zealand not to follow in their footsteps (Cullen, 1988). The push for mandatory reporting continues, however, and proposed law changes will be brought before New Zealand parliament again in 1993, despite objections from the Department of Social Welfare, who are obviously aware of the dangers.

Hotlines

In many locations in the United States and other countries, hotlines have been established. These are usually toll-free telephone lines where callers can talk anonymously to counsellors, either admitting to having been abused themselves, confessing that they have themselves abused children, or reporting suspected cases of child abuse. Hotline counsellors provide crisis counselling, referral to appropriate agencies for ongoing assistance, and reporting to the authorities of cases of suspected abuse.

Hotlines may either be operated on a permanent basis or set up in response to particular needs, usually in conjunction with television documentaries about child abuse. Televising Oprah Winfrey's child-abuse documentary "Scared Silent" lead to a massive response on hotlines, both in the United States (where the film was simulcast on three channels) and New Zealand, where over sixteen hundred calls were logged in two hours from a national population of less than four million. In the United States the response per head of population was even greater (Stirling, 1993). Subsequent referrals greatly extend the waiting lists of already overloaded helping agencies.

One of the dangers of hotlines is that where reporting is mandatory, all cases of alleged abuse given to a hotline must be reported to the authorities. There are now many records of cases where hotlines have been misused by irritated or angry neighbours, relatives or social workers (Pride, 1986; Whalen, 1991). Their usually highly advertised and toll-free status makes them readily available for prank calls. The anonymity of the telephone line means that people can make false allegations with complete immunity.

Political motivations and religious agendas

Taking a hard line against sexual abuse is likely to help win political seats and positions in high office. Various religious and political groups have their own agendas for using sexual abuse issues to effect moral or social change.

Individuals working in the field may also be motivated by specific political or religious ideology. These agendas may take precedence over what is in the best interest of the individual cases with whom they are working. Such actions may be mitigated by the belief that the end justifies the means.

From personal experience, I have seen sexual abuse and other helping agencies operating from a need to be politically correct with respect to women and minority races. They may work with the best of intentions towards redressing the balance of power in favour of the perceived oppressed group. Like many other sexual abuse agencies world-wide, the HELP Foundation in Auckland believes that sexual abuse is an act of power and control rather than of sexual expression, and that "all men are potential rapists, and all women and children potential victims". They advocate that women and girls should be counselled by women, not men.

Much of their literature and educational material emphasises the power abuse of women by men. Although this stand may have political gains in achieving more equality for women, it is not necessarily in the best interest of individual clients. I believe that teaching children that men cannot be trusted does not assist them in establishing and maintaining healthy loving relationships with the significant males in their lives.

Some of the conflict in dealing with child sexual abuse lies in an ideological and political battle over the function of family and which decisions regarding children should be made by parents or by the state. Beliefs and actions from both the far Right and the far Left contribute to a fight while what might actually be in the best interest of particular children is neglected.

Some fundamentalist Christian groups believe that sex education in schools and the provision of contraception for teenagers is part of a neo-Marxist plot to break down society's moral standards, destroy the family unit and prepare the way for violent revolution (Hughes, 1983). Providing day-care facilities in support of working mothers is viewed as part of the conspiracy to break up the family (Pride, 1986). Government policy of removing children into foster care whenever there is the slightest suspicion of parental abuse is seen as a major factor in this process.

Women's groups active in the sexual abuse field often follow socialist ideology, placing the blame for child victimisation on the capitalist system (Max, 1990). The traditional family with a male at its head is seen to restrict and control women from leading independent lives, and to mould its children to perpetuate the system.

Often groups who hold either of these belief systems when they are working with children and families will work towards achieving political and moral change in which ever direction fits their view of the world. This hidden agenda to effect social change will get in the way of the primary role of the agency or group concerned: that is the care of an individual child.

As previously discussed, minority and cult religions, and alternative communities, are often targeted by mainstream groups, motivated by disapproval or moral outrage. Their actions and reactions will often lead to premature and fallacious accusations of sexual abuse.

Child sexual abuse accommodation syndrome

Sexual abuse worker Dr Roland Summit (Summit, 1983) wrote a thesis about the effects of child sexual abuse which he labelled the Child Sexual Abuse Accommodation Syndrome (CSAAS). This has become part of mainstream teaching assumed to be verified fact.

Summit claims that sexual abuse is always accompanied by secrecy and helplessness. He theorises that abused children usually feel trapped and behave by accommodating to the situation. They might accommodate by becoming emotionally remote, being overly good, fighting with parents and being rebellious, or even developing multiple personalities. Fear results in children delaying disclosure, or telling about it in a confused and unconvincing way, and then usually retracting the story later. Summit claims that most children will never tell about abuse or seek help.

Mary Pride (Pride, 1986) summarises CSAAS in the following way:

- sexually abused children tend to contradict themselves;
- sexually abused children cover up the incident;
- sexually abused children often show no emotion after the event;
- sexually abused children often wait a long time before making their accusations.

Children who have suffered ongoing sexual abuse and told they must keep it secret may well behave in this way. However, when children who have not been abused are interrogated by adults who believe they have, they are also likely to give contradictory stories or deny the abuse, or to show no signs of being upset. Stories inadvertently created by an interrogation process are also likely to emerge long after an alleged incident.

In any circumstances other than that of sexual abuse, the above considerations would contribute to any child's story being less, not more, likely to be believed. As in a number of other areas, sexual abuse is seen to be an exception to our usual notions of sense and nonsense.

The danger of the Child Abuse Accommodation Syndrome is that whatever a child says or does can be explained as indicating that she or he has been sexually abused. This is an example of a "heads I win, tails you lose" ideology: if children say they have been abused then they have, and if they say they have not, then they still have been.

Multiple personalities

People who are diagnosed as suffering from multiple personality disorder (MPD) present themselves as possessing two or more distinct personalities, which they usually identify by different names. For example, someone suffering from the disorder may have a friendly confident personality she calls Carol, an angry one named Jo, and a meek passive one named Susan. Some of the personalities may be amnesic with regard to the others: for example, Carol may know about Susan and Jo, but Susan and Jo may claim to know nothing about the existence of the other personalities.

MPD has been an extremely rare diagnosis until recently. The condition was publicised with the popular book and film 'The Three Faces of Eve', which documented the three personalities of Chris Sizemore (Eve), and again with the book 'Sybil', which graphically described another case, believed to be the result of sadistic physical and sexual torture of Sybil as a young child. In the 1980s and 1990s television documentaries and magazine articles have continued to ensure that there is widespread public knowledge of this condition.

In the last ten years there has been a dramatic increase in diagnosing cases of MPD, almost exclusively in adults alleging abuse as children. There are some psychotherapists who make the diagnosis in many of their patients, whilst others do not see even one case in their entire career (Spanos et al, 1985). Psychotherapists who diagnose MPD often tend to view it as a survival technique adopted by children inflicted by severe abuse and inconsistent treatment from parents when very young. Some of the mainstream sexual abuse literature now suggests that MPD is a frequent outcome of childhood sexual and satanic abuse (Hechler, 1988).

Other investigators believe that the incidence has not really increased, but that people are learning to enact the role of the multiple personality patient by therapists' unwitting encouragement. Therapists may provide the information about how to enact the role with conviction, and give official validation for the various personalities enacted.

An experiment by Spanos et al (1985) resulted in nearly all their college student subjects displaying signs of multiple personality when presented with the appropriate leading questions and validation of their responses by the experimental investigator; none of the control group showed any sign of MPD. The researchers concluded that psychotherapists can play a very important part in shaping their clients' responses, and progressively encourage and validate evidence of the condition. Enacting MPD does not merely involve behaving as different people at different times; it also requires reinterpreting the past in a manner consistent with the belief of possessing more than one self.

MPD is a very convenient diagnosis where memories are only "unblocked" and recalled after therapy and hypnosis. The explanation can be given that the person adopted a different personality when undergoing abusive events, and that alternate identity was amnesic until contacted by the therapist.

Typically, MPD patients attribute to one or more of their alternate personalities behaviours of which they are ashamed, have previously denied, or which they see are uncharacteristic of them. In one famous murder case named the Hillside Strangler, the defendant Kenneth Bianchi alleged his innocence until he underwent a hypnotic interview, in which he was actively invited to "bring forth" other personalities. In this session Ken manifested evidence of multiple personality. The new personality, named Steve, claimed responsibility for the crime which he claimed Ken knew nothing about. The fact that he was suffering from MPD was used in his defence to obtain a not guilty by reason of insanity verdict.

In the United States a growing body of therapists believe in the widespread existence of satanic ritual abuse (SRA). Amongst many SRA experts, there is a belief that their adult patients are the victims of intentional, diabolical brainwashing, mind control and programmeming, and that they have had MPD deliberately conditioned by cult abusers, to prevent them remembering and disclosing the abuse. Some of these therapists believe that their clients are brainwashed satanic robots waiting to be triggered by cult leaders (Richardson et al, 1991).

In one case I know of, a young woman was diagnosed as suffering from MPD by her therapist. This young woman presented as an adolescent as outgoing, vivacious, well-presented, attractive and talented. She was popular and enjoyed being the centre of attention. Over ten years later she discovered that she was sexually abused as a teenager. After several years' intensive therapy she uncovered and manifested at least one alternate personality. Despite all her treatment, she subsequently presented as angry and bitter that she could not find the happiness available to other (non-abused) people.

Diagnosis of MPD is an extension of the belief that children who are sexually abused dissociate from the experience (Summit, 1983). The different personalities they develop are seen to be the result of desperate attempts to seal off the pain from their overwhelming trauma. To date, there is little or no scientific verification that this process actually occurs.

Munchausen Syndrome by Proxy

In 1951 a condition called Munchausen syndrome was first described in medical literature by Asher. This is a disorder in which an adult fabricates or induces a medical or psychological problem in his or her self, to gain attention from health and social services. It is named after the notorious eighteenth century Baron Von Munchausen, renowned as a teller of tall tales. Munchausen syndrome was registered as an official disorder in the Diagnostic and Statistical Manual of Mental Disorders (DSM-III) in 1980.

In 1977 a British paediatrician Roy Meadows described a condition he named Munchausen syndrome by proxy (MSP). In these cases parents or care givers fabricate or induce a physical or mental disorder in a child in their care, rather than in themselves. In MSP, the perpetrator gains attention from medical and social services personnel as the concerned caregiver of a sick child.

Classic MSP has involved making up a child's medical history, altering laboratory specimens, or inflicting physical findings on the child. Blood may be added to urine samples, rashes produced by pricking the skin, applying dyes or rubbing it with caustic substances. Children have been given poison to induce symptoms, or even infused with contaminated material into an intravenous line (Rand, 1989).

In order to maintain the deception, the adult manipulates the child to believe he or she is unwell, disabled or abused. One case has been reported of a twenty-two year old confined to a wheelchair because he had been brought up to believe he had spina bifida and could not walk - medical examination of his back and legs revealed no abnormality (Rand, 1990).

Cases are now being reported of MSP where an accusing parent or caretaker fabricates the story that a child has been abused by someone else, to enlist the support and attention of child protection workers. Mothers have been known to repeatedly present their daughters for vaginal examinations to confirm abuse, despite previous lack of findings. Children might be subjected to numerous psychological or investigative examinations, the mother moving on to other agencies and individuals when the diagnosis is not confirmed. One mother was even suspected of dilating her daughter's vagina with a tampon to produce "physical evidence" of abuse (Wakefield and Underwager, 1988).

The adult often presents a fabricated history, and frequently enlists the child's support of the story. The child will often recite allegations in a rote manner or appear eager to tell her story. Although the allegations are completely confabulated, she is likely to come to believe that she has in fact been abused. The concern and sympathy offered by sexual abuse workers, and the large number of personnel from various disciplines the adult can call on (therapists, psychologists, police, doctors, nurses, social workers) makes fabrication of abuse a likely scenario for a contemporary manifestation of MSP.

Faulty medical indicators of abuse

Much of child sexual abuse does not involve penetration, and hence diagnosis from medical signs will occur in only a minority of the cases (Lawton et al, 1987; Royal College of Physicians, 1991). The presence of sexually transmitted disease or underage pregnancy is proof of sexual activity - this is a rare finding, however.

When the vagina or anus of a young child is penetrated by a penis or fingers, bruising, tearing and bleeding is likely. Should injuries continue to occur, these orifices are likely to remain more open and show signs of scarring.

Children's genital regions have not been routinely examined in medical examinations, and until the last decade virtually nothing was written on what normal vaginas and anuses looked like in childhood (Pokorny et al, 1992; McCann et al, 1992).

In 1983, the hymens were examined and measured of nearly two hundred and fifty girls under thirteen years who were treated at a Crisis Care Unit in Denver (Cantwell, 1983). It was reported that 75% of those with horizontal openings greater than 4mm had been sexually abused. Three years later this figure was amended to 80% (Cantwell, 1986). This paper is often quoted by medical experts in court rooms and in the absence of any other studies, a horizontal hymen size greater than 4mm has been considered an indicator of sexual abuse.

Examination of this study reveals it seriously flawed, however. Firstly, the method of substantiating abuse was not clarified, and appears to include a number of girls who denied that they were victims.

Secondly, measuring hymenal size is not a simple procedure, and different examiners are likely to get different results. To establish the diameter a child's legs must be spread at the hips and the vaginal lips gently parted to expose the hymen.

Varying the amount of lateral pressure used to part the lips will distort the shape of the hymen and change the apparent diameter. Hymenal shape is very variable (Heger, 1985). Some have several openings, they may be crescent-shaped, slit-shaped (horizontal or vertical), or very irregular. The hymen might be thick and fleshy or a very thin membrane.

Not only is measurement impossible with any degree of accuracy, but Dr Raine Roberts, Manchester, reported in the British Medical Journal in 1989 that "the hymen...can vary, in the same child, from a pinhole to a centimetre, depending on whether she is relaxed or apprehensive, warm or cold". A medical finding of a dilated hymenal opening must therefore be interpreted with great caution.

The diameter of an average index or middle finger is about 20mm. An erect penis is 25 to 40mm in diameter. The hymen is not a very elastic tissue, but even allowing for some stretching, the belief that any hymenal diameter greater than 4mm is an indicator of abuse is not commonsense. The Royal College of Physicians state that a hymenal diameter of 15mm is supportive of abuse, although it should not be used as the sole basis for a diagnosis.

Unfortunately, the belief that hymenal diameters greater than 4mm indicate sexual abuse has permeated the field. I have examined a number of medical reports of vaginal examinations where hymenal sizes less than 10mm have been reported by the examining physician as indicating probable abuse.

In one particular case, a woman doctor in Christchurch, New Zealand, examined three sisters and gave the opinion that they had all probably been molested. Her examination of the five year old revealed "a transverse vaginal diameter of 5mm, and no evidence of a hymen" which she found "highly suggestive of penetration". The nine year old had a transverse vaginal opening of 3.5mm, with hymenal remnants, which she concluded was "suggestive of some interference to the vagina", and the ten year old had a transverse opening of 6mm, with no definite hymen, which she believed was "strongly indicative of vaginal penetration".

The girls were then subjected to a number of sexual abuse assessments. In her first interview session, the eldest girl was told that the doctor's examination showed that she has been the victim of "bad touching" and has a "hurt between her legs". Despite repeated questions about who has caused the "hurt", she denied any molestation. Even after two counsellors performed a role play with her about a "father who hurts kids between their legs" she was adamant that nothing like that has happened to her. Sadly she was not believed and all three children were placed in a foster home. Their father was charged with sexual violation of all his daughters, especially the eldest. It was a year and a half before his case was heard in court, where he was acquitted on all charges.

The other area of contention in medical examination regards physical signs of anal abuse. In particular, the argument centres around a phenomenon of anal gaping called the reflex anal dilatation (RAD). Briefly, this involves gently parting the buttocks and observing the anus for half a minute. Usually, the sphincter on the outside of the anus will contract and then dilate, as pressure is maintained. Sometimes the inside sphincter will then also relax giving a view right into the rectum. It is this response that has been named RAD.

British paediatricians Drs Hobbs and Wynne reported that RAD was present in 42% of anally abused children they examined, and claimed that it was an important indicator of abuse (Hobbs and Wynne, 1986; Hobbs and Wynne, 1989). They stated that they had not witnessed RAD in non-abused children. They also claimed that splits or fissures around the anus are very rare in the non-abused child.

These findings became the basis of a belief in some circles that RAD is proof of anal abuse. More recent studies and observations refute Hobbs and Wynne's findings. One study demonstrated the phenomenon in nearly half of the non-abused children they examined (McCann et al, 1989). It also appears to be more common when a child is constipated and has faeces sitting higher in the bowel (Sunderland, 1987; Royal College of Physicians, 1991). Many doctors also report that they have commonly seen anal fissures in non abused children (Freeman, 1989; Kean, 1989; Royal College of Physicians, 1991).

Unfortunately, Hobbs and Wayne's theories regarding the relevance of anal reflex dilatation was taken to be established fact by a number of doctors examining children. In some centres it became policy for all children to undergo genital and anal examinations, no matter what medical problem they had come with.

This practice resulted in the false epidemic of sexual abuse cases in Cleveland, England, which was to receive world-wide attention from the media. In 1987, two paediatricians working at the Middlesborough General Hospital in Cleveland, Drs Marietta Higgs and Geoffrey Wyatt, diagnosed one hundred and twenty-one cases of alleged sexual abuse of children in the space of five months. Their diagnoses were made largely from medical examination findings of reported hymenal irregularities and RAD. Many of these children had come to the hospital for treatment of complaints such as asthma, and there was no other evidence suggesting that they had been abused (Bernard, 1988; Woods, 1988). Dr Higgs held the view that one in ten children are sexually abused, and sincerely believed that her findings proved the abuse.

Despite denials from bewildered and distraught parents, the children were immediately taken from their homes, initially to hospital and later into care by the social services. As the numbers escalated, distressed parents sought media and political support. Eventually a public inquiry was called. The Cleveland inquiry, headed by Lord Justice Butler-Sloss, found that most of the allegations were unfounded, and the children were returned to their families. The process was however very traumatic to all concerned, and the children and their parents did not emerge unscathed by the experience.

Despite the findings of the inquiry, and the evidence coming forward from a number of reputable medical sources regarding the unreliability of relying on medical signs such as RAD to diagnose abuse, many agencies still maintain their use is valid. Dr Higgs still has many supporters within the field who believe her diagnoses were justified. Several books written about the Cleveland affair (Campbell, 1988; La Fontaine, 1990) present the view that the allegations in the Cleveland case were founded, despite overwhelming evidence that abuse was not substantiated in the vast majority of the cases.

These and many other cases show that once a belief that sexual abuse has taken place has become entrenched, very little can be done to sway the believers otherwise. To even suggest the possibility of a false allegation is often to invite an emotional outburst and accusations of condoning or even colluding with abuse.

10. Implications and Consequences of the Sexual Abuse Industry Beliefs

The values and actions of the sexual abuse industry are having ramifications in many areas of social life. Its beliefs are promulgated through extensive networking of workers, and through abuse protection programmes in state schools from preschool to tertiary levels.

Professionals who challenge mainstream sexual abuse teaching have faced threats to their careers and other persecution. In some countries everyone suspected of sexual offending is placed on a sex offender register. Subsequent acquittal does not always result in names being removed from the register, which can have serious social and employment implications for such individuals.

Claims that a quarter of all girls and a tenth of all boys are sexually abused has other social implications. A generation is emerging likely to be fearful that adults, especially men, will abuse them, and possibly interpreting loving physical contact such as hugs, pats and strokes as "bad touching". Over-emphasis on the dangers of sexual abuse is unlikely to contribute to healthy education about sexuality. There are also serious economic and social implications in imprisoning a significant and increasing percentage of the male population for sex offences.

The extreme stand taken by many in the sexual abuse industry has resulted in the so-called backlash movement. At times this takes the form of a call for the return to traditional patriarchal values and women's removal from the work force. There is also a growing body of people asking for a more moderate and rational assessment of the situation. Sadly, any challenge to the ideas promulgated by the industry are often summarily labelled as a backlash reaction and dismissed without consideration.

Effects of networking

As explained earlier in this book, the sexual abuse industry formed and grew rapidly. A large body of literature and teaching materials was quickly assembled, and there was a proliferation of seminars and training courses throughout the Western world.

A relatively small group of people (Finkelhor, Summit and Segroi, amongst others) were initially responsible for publishing what became mainstream texts and papers about sexual abuse, and further disseminated their views at workshops and international conferences. Individuals and agencies made and maintained contact for additional exchange of beliefs and ideas. These networks were quickly established both nationally and internationally, and continue to be maintained and expanded.

Networking is not new. It is a process whereby views and information are exchanged, often in an informal manner, between colleagues. Referrals within the network can also result in people being offered key jobs or resources. The "old boys' network" of the patriarchal establishment has at times justifiably been accused of favouritism and exclusiveness by feminists.

However, the development of networks are both valuable and inevitable in a modern-day world committed to the sharing of information and a cooperative approach to problem management. Networks are valuable for communication and rapid dissemination of information between people with common interests and goals. They can serve as an effective way of educating people and effecting social change.

Where the material they are spreading is unsubstantiated or faulty, however, networking can result in the widespread transmission of misinformation. Along with all the positive outcomes, erroneous or unvalidated data can rapidly become accepted as established fact. Subsequent literature based on this data will continue this distortive process, until these incorrect beliefs and erroneous information become established as irrefutable facts. This has certainly happened in the sexual abuse field, where the faulty assumptions discussed earlier in this book are generally believed to be true by both workers in the area and also the public at large.

Along with the networking amongst sexual abuse workers, there is also a substantial amount of material and information exchanged between fundamentalist church organisations. This includes the circulation of literature and videos with explicit descriptions of what contributes satanic abuse. For example, this includes enactments of people wearing robes and horns on their heads brandishing knives and dancing around fires. Such activities are presented as widespread. In the United States some church denominations even broadcast this material on their own radio and television channels. The enormous resources of these church groups is resulting in the extensive dissemination of such propaganda.

A sympathetic and comprehensive response by the media has resulted in a deluge of books, magazine and newspaper articles, videos and films about child sexual abuse. This material largely draws on the ideas and statements promoted by the networks, and further reinforces and spreads these groups' beliefs about sexual abuse.

Effects of prevention programmes

Along with all the other material discussed above, the 1980s saw the development of a large number of child sexual abuse prevention (CSAP) programmes throughout the

Western world. This programmes incorporate a variety of aids including video and audio cassettes, plays, comic and colouring books, games, films, books and instruction kits. They are widely used in daycares and pre-schools, primary, secondary and tertiary schools, churches and parents' groups, and have been developed and marketed without any research basis to their effectiveness ((Wakefield and Underwager, 1991).

The majority of these programmes are based on the belief that sexual abuse is an abuse of power, largely resulting from the inherent power imbalance between adults and children and between males and females. This ideology equates violence with sex and sees the sexual component of the abuse as a tool for the expression of power (Krivacska, 1991). There is in fact no scientific research data that validates this assumption, and indeed the available studies seem to indicate that sexual abuse of children is a form of sexual expression, where power is sometimes used as the tool (Krivacska, 1990).

Krivacska has identified several concepts that are typically found in a CSAP programme:

1. Body ownership (children's bodies belong to themselves)
2. Touch continuum (all touch is either good or bad, or sometimes there is a third category labelled "confused")
3. Secrecy (when asked to keep secrets about touch, children should tell these secrets, and secrets are different from surprises)
4. Intuition (children know intuitively what is appropriate and inappropriate touch, and these feelings should be trusted)
5. Preventive action (children can be taught to and should react to abusive situations by saying no and trying to get away)
6. Support systems (there are people available whom children can tell, and if they are not believed, they should continue to seek help from other adults)
7. Blame (children are never to blame for abuse committed against them).

Most CSAP programmes are based on these concepts and hence make a number of assumptions which are not substantiated by scientific data. Much of the teaching is liable to give children very confused and mixed messages.

There is illogical reasoning in the idea that children can be empowered to prevent abuse, promoted in conjunction with an ideology claiming that children are powerless and never responsible for abuse occurring. Children who fail to prevent abuse as they have been taught are likely to feel they are to blame.

The definition of bad touch is often confusing. If it is defined as touch that a child does not like, this means that the child's personal preference not the intent of the adult constitutes abuse. Innocent hugs and kisses from family members could be defined as abusive under this definition. Moreover, genital touching often feels pleasant to a child, and therefore may not be considered "bad touch" by a child who is taught that this is touching which "feels bad".

SAP programmes are usually introduced without the balancing influence of education on normal sexuality. Often genital body parts are only alluded to (for example, "the private parts covered by a swimming costume"). This teaches that sexual matters should not be talked about directly. Children are taught that they should scream, kick, run away and tell someone if anyone ever looks at or touches their "private parts" (apart from for washing or medical attention). A child's first introduction to sexuality may be that sex is something bad and harmful. There needs to be information on normal healthy sexuality to counterbalance this message, but school curricula often have strict restrictions from providing sex education.

Studies have revealed children who generalise the message that no-one must touch their private parts to include themselves. This means they come to believe that masturbation is taboo, and behaviours may even result such as a little boy sitting down to urinate on the toilet because he has generalised the message to include not touching his own penis (Krivaska, 1991).

We are raising a generation of children many of whom learn only about sex in terms of socially abhorrent deviant behaviour. Giving this type of information to children without teaching them about their own bodies and about developing adult sexuality in the framework of loving mutually satisfying relationships, may prevent the normal development of childhood sexuality with devastating effects at maturity.

Persecution of professionals who challenge the industry

In past eras it has been known for bearer of bad news to be put to death. These days it is more expedient to discredit them. Professionals who question some of the beliefs and opinions which are presented as undisputable facts are often accused of colluding with abuse by defending the alleged offenders, and may be blacklisted or threatened with professional deregistration.

The Cleveland case (discussed in chapter 9) is a very good example of this. One of the few medical practitioners who dared to challenge the validity of the Drs Higgs' and Wyatt's medical findings was Dr Raine Roberts from Manchester. Dr Roberts was a General Practitioner and Police surgeon specialising in sexual assault examinations. She appeared as a expert witness for the defence, and the basis of her evidence was that anal dilatation could be found in non-abused children. She also challenged the interpretation of hymenal findings.

This action made her the subject of a smear campaign by the sexual abuse industry (personal communication). She was branded a "misbeliever" who supported child sex abusers. She is mentioned in a very derogatory manner in books written about the Cleveland affair (Campbell, 1988; La Fontaine, 1990). These books present the view that the allegations in the Cleveland case were founded, despite the findings of the inquiry that the evidence was completely unsubstantiated.

Dr Ralph Underwager and his partner Hollida Wakefield are psychologists from Minnesota who have many years experience in the sexual abuse field. As well as working with clients they have extensive involvement in writing, teaching and research in this area, as well as providing expert witness evidence in court proceedings. They have questioned some of the beliefs of the industry and at times challenged allegations where they suspect the evidence to be false. They have suffered considerable persecution by the media and other professionals for this stand including a concerted campaign to destroy their professional reputations by the National Center for Prosecution of Child Abuse.

I have personally suffered a similar process, which I outline in the foreword. My action in a custody dispute and my expressed concerns about what is happening in the sexual abuse field has resulted in my being accused of "colluding with abuse". Attempts have been made to have me discredited and deregistered and I have been "blacklisted" by the professional and counselling community.

Tactics to discredit sexual abuse experts who challenge the status quo follow the general pattern of intimidation and harassment which is increasingly aimed at dissenting scientists, particularly those who testify for the defence in criminal trials. In the United States there have been a number of cases where defence scientists have been warned by the FBI not to proceed with their evidence and have been discouraged from proceeding (Kolata, 1991).

In 1991 Harvard University scientists Hartl and Lewontin submitted for publication in the journal Science a paper identifying serious flaws in DNA typing. They concluded that the current state of knowledge meant that individuals could be wrongly "matched" to forensic samples and hence incorrectly identified as offenders (Lewontin and Hartl, 1991). The researchers were pressured by the journal's editors to soften their conclusions and asked by the Criminal Justice Department to withdraw their paper because its publication could be "a disservice to the justice system". The authors reluctantly rewrote their conclusions, and the paper was not published until a solicited rebuttal was published along side (Chakraborty and Kidd, 1991). This sort of harassment undermines the basic rights of scientists to publish their research findings without censorship by parties who do not like their findings.

Sex offender registries

In the last decade databases recording details of child abuse offences have been set up in most states in America, with recent moves to establish a national central registry. Other Western countries have also been following this example. These data banks were originally aimed at identifying children who had been abused and monitoring their investigation and management. However, more recently the emphasis has shifted to recording information about the alleged offender rather than the child or family. The goal is now to prevent an abuser from ever having contact with other children who could then be abused (Underwager and Wakefield, 1991).

In the United States, the information on the registry is available to a large number of agencies including potential employers, and is required by law for certain jobs (Whalen, 1991). One of the main professed reasons for this is to prevent men who prey on children from being employed by child care centres.

Anyone suspected of child abuse is likely to have his or her name placed on a central registry. Even when the allegation is shown to be unfounded, names may stay on the registry a year or longer. Where abuse is claimed to be substantiated, names may be maintained on the list for fifty years, often without the right to appeal.

Toll-free anonymous hotlines have resulted in a number of malicious and hoax allegations of abuse. One case is reported (Whalen, 1991) of a couple in Florida, James and Mary Seay. The Seays were visited by child protection investigators after hotline allegations that they had an infant with black eyes whom they picked up by the neck and kept shut up in their bathroom. The Seays explained that their adult children had left home and that the infant was in fact their pet raccoon, and the investigators departed.

However, the bureaucratic machine was now in motion. A few days later the couple were telephoned by another agency and requested to attend for child abuse counselling. When they repeated that the "child" was a raccoon, they were told they could not be helped if they persisted in their denial and were ordered to attend counselling on threat of legal action. Eventually they managed to convince the authorities that they were victims of a hotline hoax call. By then their names were on the registry where they remained for several months as required by Florida law.

In many cases, names are only removed from the registry when a person who has been falsely accused applies for this to be done. The regulations to have a name removed or information corrected are complex, and applications may have to be made within a specified time-limit. Challenging the information on file can require persistent efforts over a long period of time. Many people who have been falsely accused may not have the educational or organisational skills, the emotional resources, or even the money to do so (Underwager and Wakefield, 1991).

Given the increasing number of false allegations of child sexual abuse, and the difficulties in getting names removed once recorded, central registries are likely to contain a significant proportion of names which should not be there (Petersen, 1991). A Child Abuse Register is essentially a blacklist, and its accessibility may result is discrimination against those appearing in it. This may include loss of jobs, harassment of children at school, having to move home, and suffering further investigation by agencies because the person is now "labelled" as an abuser.

Laws concerning such registries may be well-intentioned but have not been well thought out. Combined with the inability of bureaucracy to respond effectively to errors, and the actions of overzealous and under trained investigators, registries are likely to be instruments of injustice for many. Although intended to protect children, the potential also exists for oppression and the violation of civil rights.

Social implications

The sexual abuse industry is currently claiming that about 25% of girls and 10% of boys suffer at least one episode of sexual abuse in childhood. In general, they advocate legal and social service interventions where this occurs.

Whatever their methods of defining and identifying abuse, it is clear that what is allegedly common behaviour within our society is considered wrong and harmful by the industry. A goal that aims to investigate all such cases and provide treatment and/or legal sanctions would clearly require vast amounts of money and resources. Even if only half of the offenders were convicted and imprisoned, there would be huge economic and social impacts in having such a large percentage of the male population incarcerated.

Children and teenagers are currently being taught by their schools and the media that sexual abuse is a common danger they must watch out for. There is seldom information on healthy sexual development and adult sexuality to balance their education. This is likely to train an entire generation with distorted attitudes about sexual relationships which may have far-reaching repercussions when they mature.

The backlash movement

The extensive media coverage and popular attention to child abuse has led to some counter-reaction by individual writers and professionals. However, any challenge to mainstream thinking about sexual abuse has generally been dismissed by sexual abuse experts as a "backlash" reaction by the courts, clinics and media (Olafson, Corwin and Summit, 1993). This backlash is said to be aimed at re-suppressing awareness of sexual abuse, at least in part to reduce the cost of redressing the problem.

So-called backlash literature ranges from a fundamentalist Christian perspective (Mary Pride, 1986) through more moderate views of health professionals (Howitt, 1992; Wakefield and Underwager, 1988; Gardner, 1991) to feminist writers (Paglia, 1991). This book will no doubt be classed in that category. By dismissing challenges to its viewpoint as backlash, the industry avoids considering the many valid points and criticisms of this material.

There have even been several books written discussing the backlash phenomenon, including Susan Faludi's best-seller 'Backlash: the undeclared war against women'

(Faludi, 1992) and David Hechler's 'The battle and the backlash: the child sexual abuse war' (Hechler, 1988). Although the latter claims to be an "objective account", its emotive language is heavily biased against critics of the sexual abuse industry. The basic premise of Faludi's book is that women have yet to win the rights of "reproductive choice, equal pay, access to child care and freedom from sexual abuse" and that the backlash reaction is the male establishment reclaiming its domination over women. Faludi sees men and women at war over the issue of female independence.

The increasing numbers of falsely charged or convicted has resulted in the formation of advocacy groups which support the wrongly accused and their families. A group called VOCAL (Victims of Child Abuse Laws or Victims of Child Abuse Legislation) formed simultaneously but independently in California and Minnesota in 1984. By coincidence, both these organisations came up with the same acronym. Many major centres in the United States now have chapters of VOCAL, and similar groups have formed in Australia.

In England a similar organisation named PAIN (Parents Against INjustice) was started by families of children taken from their homes in the Cleveland cases. There are now PAIN groups in other parts of Britain and in New Zealand.

As well as supporting their members, these groups may be active in seeking legal or financial redress for the injustices they have suffered. They may also be involved in lobbying for law changes, speaking the local community, and operating a media-watch service (Schultz, 1990).

Mainstream authors seldom acknowledge that members of organisations like VOCAL have any valid cause for complaint, and often accuse them of providing the media with misleading information (Olafson, Corwin and Summit, 1993).

In general, any material, individual or group which discusses the possibility of false allegations of sexual abuse tends to be dismissed by the industry as a backlash reaction.

11. Victims rule OK?
Victimocracy and Alternative Philosophies.

"To err is human, to forgive divine"
Alexander Pope, 1711.

"To hate is easy, but it is healthier to love"
Bernie Siegel, 1986.

"Love gives naught but itself and takes naught but from itself.
Love possesses not nor would it be possessed;
For love is sufficient to love."
Kahlil Gibran, 1927.

As I discussed in the first chapter, human beings use models and paradigms to make sense of their world, and in this way create their social reality. In order for these maps of the world to be accurate they have to be revised constantly (Peck, 1978; Anderson, 1990). Being confronted with information that challenges a world view can be very threatening, even overwhelming, and many people will fiercely resist the effort required to reconstruct it. They may crusade against their maps being questioned. They may try to manipulate the world to make it conform to their view of reality. History is littered with the tragic effects of stubborn resistance to review of out-moded world views.

Where a fundamental paradigm is flawed, adherence to its basic assumptions can have serious and far-reaching consequences. This book has demonstrated some of these effects in the area of sexual abuse. One of the underlying causes of this situation can be seen if a broader view of contemporary thinking is examined.

This final chapter explores some of the evolutionary processes in human religious and political ways of seeing the world and how these affect relationships between men and women. In completion it offers a different paradigm for consideration. It discusses an alternative model for male/female relationships and looks at how this relates to work in the field of sexual abuse.

General world trend of victimology

Human beings have a long history of one group oppressing another. Discrimination may be on grounds of race, for example European colonisation of indigenous people. It may be religious, with current examples of various Christian, Moslem and Hindu sects trying to dominate or destroy one another. It may be a class discrimination, with a wealthy elite subjugating the poor, or a patriarchal society claiming men's superiority over women.

The eighteenth century saw the American Declaration of Independence in 1776 and the establishment of the first republic with the French Revolution in 1789. The basic doctrine of these movements were that all people have the same rights to freedom and equality, no matter what their race, creed or class. Human societies being what they are, however, this did not result in the elimination of all discrimination.

A century later the revolutionary German writer Karl Marx criticised the capitalist system which left the labouring class in poverty. To overcome the thousands of years of oppression and exploitation by the ruling classes for their personal enrichment, he advocated the establishment of a classless society by removing all political power from the dominant classes and preventing them getting it back (Mandel, 1979). He and fellow-writer Frederick Engels called for a *"war of the poor against the rich"* (Engels, 1969) to allow the construction of a socialist and ultimately a communist society.

Such political regimes aim at redressing the balance of power by disempowering or overthrowing the oppressor. Such a policy, still based on the concept of one group in power over another, runs substantial risks of the former victim becoming the aggressor. This is illustrated very clearly in George Orwell's 1945 cautionary tale 'Animal Farm'. In this story a group of farm animals, masterminded by the pigs, overthrow their human oppressors. Gradually the pigs assume the roles and privileges of the banished humans, eventually taking to wearing clothes and walking on their back legs, until they similarly oppress the other animals. Their revolutionary slogan *"four legs good, two legs bad"* devolves to *"four legs good, two legs better"*.

Historically, many racial, social and sexual groups have been disadvantaged by injustices. Myriads of examples include various indigenous peoples, women and homosexuals. Current social values claim that it is justifiable to redress the balance by positive discrimination. However this means that another group (the one identified as the original oppressors), is simultaneously discriminated against. I believe that such affirmative action is insulting, patronising, and demeans its recipients. Furthermore it is unfair to those discriminated against.

Ironically, programmes of positive discrimination for oppressed groups such as women or blacks perpetuate the power imbalance they claim to redress and actually maintain their victim status. Advocating protection for women or other disadvantaged groups defines them as feeble and powerless. Offering positive discrimination incentives does not enable them to achieve goals on their own merits. Moreover, for every act of positive discrimination there is a negative one (Edwards, 1993). There seems to me to be dangerous value-judgements in deciding who warrants which.

This is the age of the victim. The Western world is currently driven by this ideology of victimology. One of its basic tenets is that there are victims who need treatment and perpetrators who need punishment and correction (Money, 1991).

"We're not to blame, we're victims" is the rally-cry of a multitude of individuals and groups (Birnbaum, 1991). This practice of blaming others comes from the unrealistic expectations of our modern, risk-avoiding age. We believe we have a right to perfection and should anything in our lives fall short of this ideal, there is a strong tendency to blame whomever is seen to be in authority. In the United States this is increasingly seen as an opportunity to claim huge monetary compensations.

There are a number of advantages of being a victim in our society. As well as being discriminated for by affirmative action, being able to lay blame conveniently absolves current responsibility for a person's actions. Adult dysfunctional behaviour, be it eating disorders, addictions, or relationship problems, is frequently blamed on childhood abuse. Adults can claim that it's not their fault they're the way the are. Many celebrities are now claiming childhood abuse and being "in recovery", and glorying in the associated kudos, publicity and public sympathy. The validity of their claims is seldom questioned and they are heralded for their bravery and frankness in confessing their traumatic childhoods to the world.

The philosophy of victimology invites a society of children. Rewards are offered for being a victim, and autonomous adulthood appears to have little going for it. Wherever someone suffers from an imbalance of power (for example, from being female, darker-skinned, gay, younger, or in a inferior position with respect to education or employment) it seems they can claim diminished responsibility for their actions.

Protecting the rights of potential victims is taken to more and more ludicrous proportions. The politically correct must be careful not to practise racism, sexism, classism, homophobia or discrimination of the disabled. Now they must also watch their step with respect to "lookism", and not respond differently to people because of how they look.

The Californian town Santa Cruz recently passed a law prohibiting discrimination on the grounds of physical appearance. The law was written after a woman weighing 135 kilograms was denied a job at a health food shop because the owner felt she would be a poor advertisement for health foods. The city council now legislate against "uglyism", and forbid job or housing discrimination on the basis of what people look like (Reed, 1992). Amongst other things, this could put casting agencies for models and actors in a very difficult position.

Victimology has lead to much career-building in the past couple of decades, and not just in the child abuse field. There are support-groups for sufferers from every conceivable disability or disadvantage. Many cities have refuges for battered women. There are many lawyers who have got very rich defending the rights of victims.

New Zealand has recently set up a government-appointed Victims Task Force which oversees services and information for victims of crime and provides funding to victim support groups. It produces a Victim Impact Statement to be used during a trial and sentencing, and will provide notification upon request to victims of when their offender is released from prison. It also invites victims to write to parole boards letting them know how they feel about offenders getting parole.

Even violent perpetrators may try to absolve themselves from responsibility for their behaviour on the grounds that they themselves were abused as children. One of our prevailing myths is that violence begets violence. However the empirical evidence for this is slim - current research demonstrates that the majority of adult abusers were not abused in their own childhood (Widom, 1989).

Human societies have a history of violence throughout time. There always exists the inherent conflict between the rights of the individual to do what he or she wishes and that which is in the best interest of the social group. We are simultaneously social animals, members of a herd who follow a leader, and autonomous individuals with choices and free-will. Various cultures address this problem in different ways, with controls and regulations enabling groups of people to function co-operatively and harmoniously.

This will often effectively limit interpersonal violence within the group, but does allow for the possibility of one group oppressing or overpowering another.

Modern societies are witnessing an escalation in interpersonal violence. There are many factors contributing to the cause of this. There is a breakdown in traditional cultural values and restraints as the world's races and religions intermingle internationally. Ideologies of equality have led to unrealistic expectations for all to be healthy and wealthy. Worsening poverty and unemployment results in increasing anger and resentment and contributes to social violence. Over-population and human competition for ever-shrinking territory and resources compounds this.

Television and other forms of media are another contributing factor to current levels of social aggression. A growing body of evidence suggests that heavy television viewing can lead to a distorted perception about real-life violence in both adults and children (Slaby and Quarforth, 1986), and that watching TV violence can lead to increased levels of aggression (Wilson and Herrnstein, 1985).

Male oppressor/female victim

Feminist ideology has reacted to the traditional male monopoly of social and political power, and quite appropriately sought to redress excessive power imbalances between men and women. Women have achieved huge gains in sharing some of this power over the last century. Gaining the vote and obtaining increased educational and employment opportunities has give many women more chances to take control of their own lives.

Feminist politics have some of their roots in Marxist principles. Sometimes this is manifest by a philosophy which defines its reality as a battle between the sexes. It calls for women to seize power from men. Certainly women must still strive to obtain and maintain equalities with men. However a model which places men and women as adversaries fosters mistrust, and is unlikely to result in equal and harmonious relationships between them.

What started with the Suffragettes and continued with Women's Liberation as a movement to empower women, has devolved into an ideology of blame. To quote Camille Paglia, a provocative feminist writer of the 1990s: *"The current movement has declined into smug formulas and codes of political correctness. What began as a movement of eccentric individualists has turned into an ideology that attracts weak personalities who are looking for something to believe in. Or someone to blame."* (Paglia, 1990).

When men are blamed for social inequalities, women do not take responsibility for their circumstances and may identify themselves as victims. Their response is anger or even hatred towards their male oppressors. However being constantly angry has a high cost physically, emotionally and mentally. As American therapist and writer Anne Wilson Schaef recognises, *"victims don't get better - they get bitter"* (Schaef, 1992).

Mainstream sexual abuse counselling claims that forgiveness of the abuser is not an essential part of the healing process. In 'The Courage to Heal', which is often prescribed as a vital text for both counsellors and clients to read, it states that 'giving up your anger and blame is not part of healing.... never say or imply that the client should forgive the abuser. If you hold the belief that survivors should forgive the abuser in order to heal, you should not be working with survivors' (Bass and Davis, 1988).

In this model of the world, women are encouraged to mobilise their anger and outrage against the domination of men. When male/female relationships are viewed this way, many women find it extremely difficult for men to "do it right" for them. Assertive behaviour by men is likely to be considered unacceptably dominating or "macho". However, men who respond by trying to be non-assertive and eager to please are often seen as wimps, and do not command women's respect.

Forgiveness, compassion and love

Most of the world's great religions are founded on concepts of forgiveness and love. Buddhism teaches its followers to do no harm, neither to themselves nor others. Confucius advocated humaneness, which he said was "to love others" (Dawson, 1986).

"Love your neighbour" has always been the "Golden Rule" of Judaism. Early

Rabbinic master Hillel is quoted as saying *"That which is hateful to you, do not do to your neighbour. This is the entire Torah; the rest is commentary - go and learn it"* (Babylonian Talmud, Shabbat 31a).

Jesus was a Jewish teacher and it is therefore not surprising that Christianity adopted this basic Judaic doctrine of "love thy neighbour as thyself". In particular, Jesus commanded his followers to love their enemies and pray for their persecutors, to *"forgive, and ye shall be forgiven"* (New Testament, Matt. 5.43-7; Lk 6.27-38). Love and compassion of each other is love of God (*"if we love one another, God dwells in us"*, 1 Jn 4.12). Even crucified on the cross, Jesus still preached forgiveness (*"Father, forgive them; for they know not what they do"*, Lk 23. 34).

This message is again repeated in Islamic law: *"None of you has faith unless he loves for his brother what he loves for himself"* (Hadrith [Bukhari] 2:6).

Jesus' message was about a loving God, who should be celebrated with praise, thanks and blessing. Human beings were not born sinners, but only became so through their own actions, for which they were individually responsible.

The concept of original sin was introduced by St Augustine in the 4th century. Much of his teachings were based on Greek philosophy which claimed that the spiritual was immaterial and asensual (Fox, 1981). Within this doctrine was the message that human sensuality is sinful. Augustine developed the notion of redemption theology. People were to reject the pleasures of the flesh, and atone for their sins through suffering. A basic tenet of subsequent Christianity was an overwhelming disapproval of the pleasures of sex - sexuality should be only for the purposes of reproduction, and its use for any other ends, such as pleasure, was abuse (Aries and Bejin, 1985).

Fall/redemption theology is based on dualism, on a separation between mind and body, between spirituality and sensuality. Modern Christianity still adheres to dualistic ways of thinking, which has pervaded Western consciousness for the last one and a half millennia. Such a belief system is driven by blame and guilt. Dividing people into oppressors and victims is a typical example of dualistic thinking.

Dualism empowers the Church and other authorities promoting it, but disempowers the people (Fox, 1979). This is being increasingly recognised by many writers. Contemporary feminist therapist Anne Wilson Schaef writes *"when we set up dualism such as mind-body, we deny the possibility of their interacting"* (Schaef, 1992).

Radical Dominican priest Matthew Fox advocates a theology based on original blessing, where dualistic "either/or" consciousness is replaced by a "both/and" dialectic way of thinking and being. In his model of the world, we should celebrate the blessings of life. His is a spirituality based on compassion, of passion put to the use of celebrating and healing (Fox, 1990). He sees pleasure as a deeply spiritual experience, ecstasy as the experience of God.

Such a creation-based spirituality empowers the individual. This path to healing through forgiveness, compassion, and love is recognised by many writers and therapists. We forgive and heal ourselves to the extent we forgive others. Much of our suffering, our victimisation, is self-inflicted. In the words of Kahlil Gibran:

"And could you keep your heart in wonder at the daily miracles of your life, your pain would not seem less wondrous than your joy;...
Much of your pain is self-chosen" (Gibran, 1926).

Mobilising anger and outrage may be an initial part of the therapeutic process, but revenge and retribution do not promote healing nor empower an individual. I believe that therapy should ultimately aim for forgiveness of both offender and self. This is diametrically opposed to the mainstream belief of the sexual abuse industry that there is no place for forgiveness in sexual abuse therapy.

It should be emphasised that forgiving those who have offended against you does not mean you condone their offensive behaviour. Furthermore, forgiving them is in your own best interest, not theirs.

American surgeon Bernie Siegel describes how forgiving those who have wronged you can release the healing power of love (Siegel, 1986).

Psychiatrist Scott Peck writes:

"The essential ingredient of successful deep and meaningful psychotherapy is love... the process of psychotherapy ultimately requires one to assume total responsibility for one's condition .. there is no longer anyone to blame.. and what was once perceived as problems are now seen as opportunities or lessons." (Peck, 1978).

Therapist Charlotte Kasl expresses a similar sentiment:

"Healing comes from affirming one's power, from learning to make self affirming choices and having the strength to love oneself no matter what another person says or does. By relinquishing hate, one breaks the negative tie to the abuser. It is a terrifying step to see in our own hearts the mirror of our abuser. Yet in doing so we begin to accept our humanness which is the source of forgiveness." (Kasl, 1986).

Sexual abuse and other areas of victim oppression are often expressed as issues of power abuse. Power is neither inherently good nor evil - it is an inescapable aspect of all human relationships and can be used or misused. There will usually be an inequality of power in any one interaction, although these imbalances may even out over time. The greater the imbalance of power, the greater the capacity for its misuse, but misuse is not inevitable. (Toffler, 1990).

A dualistic view of the world focuses on one individual or group having power **over** an other. Empowering a person does not necessarily give him or her power over others, however. We also need to consider "power-from-within", the *"acts of creation and connection, of planting, building, writing, cleaning, healing, soothing, playing, singing and making love which sustain our lives"* (Starhawk, 1987). Another aspect of personal power is our "power-with", our ability to take responsibility and influence others by their willingness to listen to our ideas. Feeling responsible for our selves, free from guilt and blame, is truly empowering.

Therapists who support their clients identifying themselves as victims are creating and maintaining a position of power over them. Dependency on one's counsellor does not promote self-responsibility and self-esteem. Anne Wilson Schaef claims that: *"psychotherapists have become victims of their own world view, belief system, and disease"* (Schaef, 1992).

More and more health professionals are questioning the scientific biomedical model of disease on which modern medicine is based. The idea that physical and mental diseases are separate entities is becoming outdated, and it is being recognised that personality, life experiences, relationships and environment all influence health and illness (Engel, 1974).

The modern proliferation of "health" practitioners and "health" shops, and a thriving self-improvement industry reflects an increasing awareness in the holistic aspects of health care. Many alternative practitioners may make claims unsubstantiated by scientific evidence; much of what they offer relates to the amount of positive attention, support and time they give their clients.

A therapist's role can be viewed as mobilising his or her clients to have an active role in their own healing (Engel, 1988). This may be to facilitate them to tell their stories, feel listened to, and reframe their life experiences in positive ways that work for them. We are each the story of our lives (Brody, 1987) - this is the basis of our self-understanding. Our narratives give our lives meaning, providing a framework for interpreting events, ordering them into intelligible patterns, and providing an ongoing sequence in time and place.

Therapy which places responsibility for health and healing in the client's hands, and does not foster dependency, is truly empowering.

Alternative model of female/male relationships

Throughout virtually all of recordable history, most cultures have held women in a subordinate position to men. This has been particularly so with respect to property, government, education and occupation. These are some of the areas which have been substantially redressed by feminism in the last century.

Not all women have been completely powerless in the past however, and in many societies women have had considerable control and influence in certain spheres, particularly social and domestic ones. In parallel with the concept of a patriarch in charge of household, there are also many historical examples of husband and wife as equal partners, each with their own specialised roles in family life.

Jewish women have traditionally enjoyed much power within the home and in child-rearing. Judaism has always acknowledged marriage as a partnership. During the weekly Shabbat ritual, a husband re-declares his love for his wife, and his appreciation for the work she does (Siegel et al, 1973).

The Roman poet Ovid advised two thousand years ago: *"If thy would marry wisely, marry thy equal."*

This century has seen a swing in the pendulum of social change for women. The Suffragette and Women's Liberation movements gave women massive advances with respect to their freedom and equality with men. This could be seen to have culminated in the 1970s as expressed in a popular song 'I am woman.. I am invincible'. The 1990s have seen a partial return to women being powerless, epitomised by the catch-cry 'all women are potential victims'.

As discussed above, much modern feminism, and particularly within the field of sexual abuse therapy, advocates an adversarial relationship of women with men. Women who have seen themselves as subjugated by men are encouraged to replace submissive behaviour with angry aggressive action, to move from a position of dependency to independence from men.

This analysis is of a world where men are the winners and women the losers, and what is recommended is turning the tables, so that women can win over men. Such a philosophy inevitably results in mistrust between women and men.

I believe an alternative way of redressing the imbalance is as a win/win situation, where male/female relationships are not viewed as a battle between the sexes. Couples need to see each other as equal members of a team, partners who are both on the same side.

It must be explained that equal does not necessarily mean the same. The genetic difference between women and men is about three percent, but this produces significant physical, mental and emotional differences between the sexes which should not be denied. The concept of masculinity or femininity is another example of dualism. In fact, we all have both components, but most human beings have a predominance of one or the other, resulting in their identifying as either male or female.

Modern society has significantly challenged and disrupted traditional male and female roles and values. This has given women significant gains with respect to their equality, but it has also resulted in a paucity of role models for both sexes. We need to learn how to be men and women in today's world, and how to establish and maintain healthy relationships with each other.

Rather than focusing on the dualistic idea of submissive or aggressive behaviour, both women and men need to learn to be assertive. Assertive behaviour involves identifying what you want, and giving clear and direct messages to each other about it, without unreasonable expectations that the other must do what you want. Ultimately, it involves taking full responsibility to what happens to you in your relationship and in your life.

Assertive behaviour has not been part of the traditional view of femininity as receptive and passive. Women have taken great strides in learning to be assertive in the past few decades, and slowly positive models have been emerging through education and the media of strong self-assured women.

Assertive women can be very threatening to men, who have not learned appropriate new ways of responding. The New Age man who tries to do it right for women by abandoning his aggressive dominant behaviour will often also let go of the forceful and heroic aspects of his masculinity. There has been a recent emergence of a men's movement whereby men rediscover their masculinity and search for appropriate role models for modern men.

Men's group leader and writer Robert Bly claims men need to rediscover the wild man, the warrior in themselves (Bly, 1990). A warrior is not afraid to show his sword, but this does not mean he will use it without just cause. He uses aggression only to defend his rightful space. Wanton violence is not a function but a dysfunction of masculinity - it is what a man does when all else has failed. Beating women and children is not the act of a warrior.

A truly confident and self-assured man knows how to be strong and assertive, but is also comfortable with the more feminine, soft and gentle aspects of himself. Similarly, a woman needs to retain her receptive empathic nature whilst developing her ability to act assertively and effectively.

A healthy relationship between women and men is one where neither is dependent on the other, but there is the interdependency of a partnership. Both partners approach the relationship as autonomous individuals in their own right, strong in their sense of self.

Psychiatrist Scott Peck has this to say on loving relationships:

"We are incapable of love unless we love ourselves .. love is the free exercise of choice ... two people love each other only when they are quite capable of living without each other but choose to live with each other." (Peck, 1978).

The concept of interdependence within marriage is even more powerfully expressed in the poetry of Kahlil Gibran:

"Let there be spaces in your togetherness.
And let the winds of the heavens dance between you.
Love one another, but make not a bond of love:
Let it rather be a moving sea between the shores of your souls...
Give your hearts, but not into each other's keeping." (Gibran, 1926).

As we move towards the twenty-first century, we have the opportunity for both women and men to know and to extend themselves as self-governing, balanced and rounded individuals. From here there is the possibility for the development of trusting, loving, co-operative relationships.

I believe that both as individuals and as a species, mankind is headed on a path of spiritual progress. Certainly there is a history of violence throughout human history.

Individuals and groups have overpowered each other in attempts to protect their territory and their models of the world. However, despite man's violent urges, I believe there is a general trend towards human spiritual evolution.

It seems to me that human beings are no more evil now than they have been at other times in history. In fact, there is often a willingness to look for solutions to social problems, moves towards more humane practices and more rational ways of operating. Slavery of other people is no longer considered acceptable to mankind. Nor is the misuse of child labour, as epitomised by boy chimney sweeps during the Victorian era.

Quite rightly, abuse of children, be it physical, emotional or sexual, is no longer condoned. As a society, we do need to protect our children against violation. In our urgency to redress these wrongs, other evils have been inadvertently created in the process. This book represents part of a growing awareness of the extreme reaction of the sexual abuse industry, and a move towards more balance in our response.

Appendix:
Ways the problems can be redressed

Whenever we intervene in the lives of children and their families, it is important that our primary consideration is "first do no harm". We require strategies that can effectively identify and manage children who have been abused with the least negative sequelae from the process. These procedures need to detect and deal with as many abused children as possible while minimising the erroneous diagnosis of non-abused children as abused.

The effects of false allegations on children, the accused and their families need to be evaluated. The harmful effects of inappropriate interventions (such as giving a non-abused child sexual abuse therapy) must be recognised, and actions neither taken lightly nor rashly.

This book has been very critical of some of the beliefs and actions of workers in the sexual abuse field. I would like to emphasis that within the system there are many instances where children are found to be abused and they are given protection and appropriate support and care. Sexual abuse workers operate with the very best of intentions. Children are now being assisted where two decades ago they had little chance of help.

This appendix addresses what I see as the specific shortfalls of the system, with brief suggestions as to how these errors or failings might be remedied by different workers and professional groups within the field.

Research

One of my primary criticisms of the sexual abuse industry is its general reluctance to address challenge. Policies and procedures should be determined by professional and clinical scientific studies, and not be politically or morally driven. Safe-guards are required so that attitudes and beliefs such as those presented in the officially recommended text "Courage to Heal" (Bass and Davis, 1988) are not accepted as proven facts without careful evaluation.

Too often in this field, theories and beliefs have become lore and been established as facts without any objective validation. For example, Roland Summit's "sexual abuse accommodation syndrome" is assumed to be valid without scientific verification. Subsequent literature and teaching perpetuate the fallacious assumptions that this data is proven. The teaching and practice of sexual abuse workers needs ongoing quality assessment and should be open to challenge, evaluation and review.

Research data available from a variety of academic sources, especially research information on the nature of memory and suggestibility, needs to be readily available to workers in the field. Academic and professional models of research and evaluation should not be dismissed as the trappings of a patriarchal society, but accepted as valid and useful tools. Research is necessary to assess that overall, what we are doing is of benefit, and not causing harm.

Ongoing studies are vital in a large number of areas in this field. We need to know what is normal behaviour within childhood and in families within specific cultures. We require knowledge of the probabilities of specific behaviours or actions being beneficial or harmful. We need this information about both the people with whom we are working and also about our own interventions. As much as possible, we must avoid making premature assumptions about these effects.

For example, when studying possible sequelae of sexual activities in childhood, the protocol should not define all child/adult sexual contacts as inevitably harmful and abusive. Positive and negative outcomes can be offered as a continuum without any judgements being made by the researcher.

Education

The primary function of education can be considered to be the transmission of values. We should assess how society transmits these values with respect to sexuality.

Sexual abuse prevention programmes need to be carefully evaluated as to the messages they are teaching with regard to sexuality. Healthy role models based on mutual respect and trust are likely to reduce the incidence of coercive sexual behaviour.

There should be baseline studies and evaluation of the effectiveness of prevention programmes before they are introduced into schools. Concepts such as "good" and "bad" touching and children knowing intuitively what is appropriate or inappropriate touching should not be introduced without scientific substantiation.

Professionals working in this field need specialised training using proven data and techniques. People should be carefully screened to minimise the possibility of their moral or political beliefs influencing their work. Course material needs ongoing scrutiny and upgrading as research and other information become available, and should be open to challenge and review.

The disturbing nature of sexual abuse work means it is particularly important for

Diagnosis of sexual abuse

Interrogation of children alleged to have been sexually abused should only be carried out by trained and experienced professionals, whether they be social workers, psychologists or police. These investigators should have adequate knowledge and understanding regarding the nature of memory recall and the effects of suggestibility contaminating any evidence.

They must appreciate that a prior belief on the part of an interviewer that the child has been abused is extremely likely to influence the findings of the investigation. Any worker who dogmatically asserts that "children never lie" about abuse, and defines him or herself as a 'validator', should not be employed to perform diagnostic interviews.

It should be acknowledged that there may be motives for false allegations being made, and this possibility needs to be considered, especially in cases such as custody battles.

Diagnostic aids, including anatomically-correct dolls, need vigorous testing before they are accepted as valid diagnostic tools. There needs to be comparisons made with baseline studies to see how non-abused children respond to them.

Great care must be used interpreting "behavioural indicators" of sexual abuse. It should be acknowledged that sexual abuse is only one of many causes of these behaviours, and may not be the most likely. All children will exhibit some of these behaviours at some time or other.

Disclosure interviews should be conducted by trained experienced personnel who strive to minimise distorted information being produced. They must appreciate how children who are eager to please can be easily cued by leading gestures, questions and stimuli. These interviews should take place before the child is informally questioned to any degree. All interviews should be videotaped and the alleged offender as well as non-accused care givers should have access to the tapes.

The negative effects of the investigation need to be recognised, with attempts to minimise the possible trauma and long-term sequelae that can be associated with the process. Moreover, such an investigation should not be embarked upon lightly, as its effects on a non-abused child is likely to be damaging. Common sense should prevail when considering where allegations should be investigated, and mandatory reporting of all suspicions of abuse is inappropriate. Current cut-backs in health, education and social welfare support to the under-privileged means we must make the most effective use of public money. Policies that increase the number of false allegations being reported are a tragic misuse of our limited resources.

Medical procedures

The medical profession should be very cautious about acting on new information regarding diagnosis and treatment until it has been adequately evaluated. Papers claiming diagnostic markers such as hymen size and anal reflex dilatation should be carefully assessed by doctors as to their validity, and the research used to establish them. Doctors should avoid making fashionable diagnoses such as multiple personality syndrome without scientific verification of its validity.

There should be support for doctors who question some of the information disseminated by the sexual abuse network. Doctors who consider the possibility of an allegation being false should not have to face charges of colluding with abuse. They should be able to openly challenge the system when appropriate without fear of blacklisting and professional discreditation.

Police procedures

The primary concern in a sexual abuse investigation, as with other alleged crimes, is that the police investigate with an open mind. It should be remembered that all alleged offenders, including sex offenders, are supposed to be considered innocent until proven guilty.

When someone who is accused of a sexual offence denies it, it is the purpose of the investigation to establish his or her innocence or otherwise. The person who denies the allegation should not be assumed. guilty. by the police without a fair trial, and should not be subjected to police pressure to "confess".

When the decision is made to investigate an allegation, the child should be interviewed by a skilled, experienced professional, either from the police force or from assistant social services. This person's training should meet the guidelines discussed previously.

Courtroom practices

The courts need to recognise the changing nature of memory. Extreme care needs to be taken when evidence relies solely on reported memories, and it should be acknowledged that neither version may be historically accurate.

The courts should also recognise that a witnesses who provide a lot of details in their evidence, especially about trivial issues, are in fact less likely to be accurate about the central event than those with a poor memory for peripheral details. Jurors should be given this information.

Courts of law usually maintain that criminal defendants are innocent until proven guilty. However there is currently a practical presumption of guilt in child abuse cases, if the belief that "children don't lie about abuse" is upheld.

places, children's out of court statements are admitted as evidence even though they are only hearsay. Only in child abuse allegations are children considered as competent to testify as witnesses. Only in such cases may witnesses give evidence without having to face their accused. In all other crimes, an alleged offender has the right to confront his accuser in the courtroom. He cannot be convicted on the uncorroborated hearsay evidence of a child.

These special rules of prosecution have been introduced with the best of intentions. Usually there is no witness and no physical evidence when sexual abuse has occurred. It is widely believed that it would be traumatic and harmful for a child to face the accused in court, although this has not in fact been substantiated by the research to date. In endeavouring to protect children, however, the rights of the defendant. to a fair trial have been seriously compromised. No-one should ever be convicted when the evidence rests solely on uncorroborated reported memories.

One of the most valuable measures that has been introduced in the courtroom is the use of videotaped disclosure interviews of children. Given the ease by which unskilled interviewing of a child can distort the evidence, it is vital that the child is interrogated by an experienced expert at the onset of the investigation. *All* disclosure interviews, not just the final one, should be videotaped and made available to the court. The defendant should have the opportunity to have this material examined by an independent expert to assess the likelihood of the interview process having created or distorted the child's story.

The current situation, where experts do not dare to suggest the possibility of an allegation being false for fear of being blacklisted, needs to be redressed. The courts urgently require the services of professionals who view the field with an open mind and are not driven by moral or political ideologies.

Treatment of sexual abuse victims

All therapeutic techniques should be assessed with respect to their effectiveness. Therapy which does not meet such criteria should not be practised, and certainly not publicly funded. In the field of medicine, new drug treatments are never introduced without extensive testing of their effectiveness and their side-effects. These same principles should apply to all psychological therapy. Funding is required for appropriate studies and trials rather than taking unevaluated theories on board.

Therapists require specialised training. It needs to be recognised that victims of sexual abuse are not likely to be the best therapists, as personal issues are more likely to interfere with their ability to provide effective therapy.

As with those working with disclosure of abuse, therapists need a healthy scepticism when looking at the content of the allegations. They should recognise the processes by which their clients have come to recall their particular stories. In the vast processes by which their clients have come to recall their particular stories. In the vast majority of cases, there is no way for a therapist to know whether what is claimed to have happened is historically accurate. A therapist can still help a client work with these stories however, by accepting them as metaphors of his or her experience. This validates a person's feelings about a past memory, without necessarily knowing whether it really did occur.

The goal of therapy should be to enable clients to work through their pain, shame and blame, and take control of their own lives, to promote self-responsibility and self-esteem. Therapy should model and support the development of loving, trusting, intimate relationships. Teaching women that men are to be distrusted and feared is unlikely to assist in this aim.

Counsellors and therapists should not assist their clients to reframe their past experiences as having been harmful. If clients believe that sexual activities they experienced as children were enjoyable, the therapist should support them in that belief. Convincing them that it was really bad and traumatic does not promote their mental health.

Treatment of offenders

It may well be more appropriate to use a medical rather than a legal model in dealing with offenders. There are very few cases where punitive incarceration has been demonstrated to prevent reoffending. Prisons operate on a submissive/aggressive behaviour paradigm. The model prisoner does what he is told. There is no place for him to practise assertive behaviour, and the concept of dominating behaviour (as modelled by the guards) equating power is reinforced.

If a man has engaged in abusive behaviour because he has felt powerless and inadequate in his life, it seems unlikely that placing him in a position of complete powerless in jail will assist him in feeling in control of his life on his release. Residivicism rates of sex offenders confirm this.

Offenders require programmes that empower them as individuals and offer them strategies for dealing with those occasions when they feel powerless and out of control. Anger management courses, which are becoming more prevalent, are starting to address some of these issues.

Treatment of offenders should be directed at encouraging, teaching and assisting them to form healthy sexual relationships. Locking men away with no sexual outlets, and no conjugal visits, is not going to assist them in developing loving sexual relationships. Many of those who are in relationships when they enter prison are likely to find themselves single by the time they are released.

There should be more work done on using a therapeutic approach in dealing with incest. There are now a few programmes which treat incestuous families by working with the whole family, if the man and woman decide they want to keep the relationship and the family together (McCarthy, 1990). Such therapy aims to restore the bond of respect, trust and intimacy between the parents. Each family member must assume responsibility for his or her behaviour, including sexual behaviour, and the family is restructured to prevent further inappropriate sexual activities recurring. The treatment is formally terminated by an apology from the offender and the non protecting parent. The children are told that once they have accepted the apology, they may no longer use incest as a way of asserting power, blame or control in the family.

Such a model aims at establishing a healthy functioning family. The offender maintains relationships with his wife and children. The children are able to work through the issues so that they do not remain victims who blame their adult misfortunes on childhood experiences. They are able to continue a relationship with their father, hopefully improved. They do not have to deal with the guilt and ambivalent feelings often associated with their father going to prison as a result of their charges.

Legal considerations

When considering the definition of sexual abuse, the law needs to consider the intent, context and effects of particular actions. This should include an understanding of the cultural meanings of certain behaviours.

It should be recognised that a very large percentage of young people are sexually active before the age of consent, and the implications of maintaining an unenforceable law on the books should be seriously considered.

People wrongly accused should have some legal redress, particularly where there were deliberate attempts to mislead on behalf of the accuser. In custody battles, there is a strong case for custody to be given to the falsely accused parent with only supervised access for the accusing parent. Ordering the latter to pay court costs may also be appropriate. In Russia, the false accuser may be ordered to serve the same penalty as the accused.

The Media

People who work in the media must recognise the power they have in disseminating myths and misinformation, and in shaping public beliefs and attitudes. It is easy to fuel the hysteria when dealing with such an emotional area as sexual abuse.

The media should continually examine and question the validity of its information and try to avoid the pitfall of rejecting unpopular but accurate information by discrediting its source. Reporters should not regurgitate public relation releases from political organisations without verification and offering a balancing point of view.

Journalists and other public communicators should acknowledge that the picture they present is inevitably coloured by observer bias. However, they should strive for objectivity, and not allow political or popular pressure to influence what they present.

Two decades ago, sexual abuse was under-reported and under-investigated. In our attempts to recognise and deal with the problem, strategies have resulted in the other extreme. It is now time to reach a balance, where attempts to diagnose and deal with sexual abuse are off-set by trying to minimise the consequences of investigating false allegations.

References

American Medical Association (1985). 'Diagnosis and treatment guidelines concerning child abuse and neglect', *Journal of the American Medical Association*, 254, 796-800.
Anderson Christopher (19 Dec 1991). 'DNA fingerprinting discord', *Nature*, 354, 500.
Anderson Walter Truett (1990). *Reality isn't what it used to be*, Harper Collins, New York.
Aries, Phillippe (1962). *Centuries of childhood*, Penguin Books, Harmondsworth.
Aries Phiippe; Bejun Andre (1985). *Western sexuality: practice and precept in past and present times*, Basil Blackwell, Oxford.
Asimov Isaac (1987). *The roving mind*, Oxford University Press.
Bachmann G, Moeller T, Benett J (Apr 1988). 'Childhood Sexual Abuse and the Consequences in Adult Women', *Obstetrics and Gynaecology*, 71 (4), 631-42.
Bass Ellen, Davis, Laura (1988). *The Courage to heal: a guide for women survivors of sexual abuse*, Harper and Row, New York.
Bell B, Loftus E (1989). 'Trivial persuasion in the courtroom: the power of (a few) minor details', *Journal of Personality and Social Psychology* 56(50, 669-679).
Bell B, Loftus E (1988). 'Degree of detail of eyewitness testimony and mock juror judgements', *Journal of Applied Social Psychology* 18(14), 1171-1192.
Benedek E, Schetky D (1987). 'Problems in validating allegations of sexual abuse. Part I: factors affecting perception and recall of events', *Journal of American Academy of Child and Adolescent Psychiatry* 26(6) 912-916.
Bentovim A (1977). 'The diagnosis of child sexual abuse,' *Bulletin of Royal College of Psychiatrists* 11:295-9.
Ben-Yehuda Nachman (1990). *The politics and morality of deviance*, State University of New York Press.
Bernard V A (16 July 1988). 'Implications of the Cleveland child inquiry: child sexual abuse demands cooperation', *British Medical Journal*, 297, 151-2.
Besharov Douglas (Nov/Dec 1985). 'An overdose of concern: child abuse and the over-reporting problem', *Regulation: AEI Journal on Government and Society*, 25-8.
Birnbaum Jesse (12 Aug 1991). 'Crybabies: eternal victims', *Time*, 38-40.
Blush Gordon, Ross Karol (1990). 'Investigation and case management issues and strategies', *Issues in Child Abuse Accusations*, 2 (3), 152-60.
Bly Robert (1990). *Iron John*, Addison-Wesley Publishing Co.
Bonanno G (Summer 1990). 'Remembering and Psychotherapy', *Psychotherapy* 27 (2), 175-86.
Brant R, Tisza V (Jan 1977). 'The sexually abused child', *American Journal of Orthopsychiatry* 47(1), 80-90.
Bravos, Zachary (1991). 'Child abuse and witchcraft? Perspective on the 15th and 20th centuries', *Issues in Child Abuse Accusations*, 3 (3), 144-153.
Brehmer B (1980). 'In one word: not from experience', *Acta Psychologica* 45, 223-241.

Bresee Patricia, Stearns Geoffrey, Bess Bruce, Packer Leslie (Feb 1986). 'Allegations of child sexual abuse in child custody disputes: a therapeutic assessment model', *American Journal of Orthopsychiatry*, 56 (4), 560-9.

Brody Howard (1987). *Stories of sickness*, Yale University Press, New Haven and London.

Brongersma Edward (Feb 1988). 'A defence of sexual liberty for all ages', *The Howard Journal* 27 (1), 32-43.

Buckey P, Buckey R, Buckey P A (1991). 'After the McMartin trials: some reflections from the Buckeys', *Issues in Child Abuse Accusations*, 2 (4), 220-5.

Bull R (1989).'Can training enhance the detection of deception?', In Yuille, J. *Credibility Assessment*, Kluwer Publishers, 83-99.

Campbell Beatrix (1988). *Unofficial secrets. Child sexual abuse: the Cleveland case*, Virago Press, London.

Cantwell Hendrika (1987). 'Update on vaginal inspection as it relates to child sexual abuse in girls under thirteen', *Child Abuse and Neglect*, 11, 545.

Caplan Pat, Ed (1987). *The cultural construction of sexuality*, Tavistock Publications, England.

Ceci Stephen, Bruck Maggie (May 1992). The suggestibility of the child witness: a historical review and synthesis', of children's memory: psycholegal implications', *Journal of Experimental Psychology: General* 116(1), 38-49.

Ceci S, Ross D, Toglia M (1988).'On remembering...more or less: a trace strength interpretation of developmental differences in suggestibility', *Journal of Experimental Psychology: General* 117(2), 201-203.

Chakraborty Ranajit, Kidd Kenneth (20 Dec 1991). 'The utility of DNA typing in forensic work', *Science*, 254, 1735-9.

Cole W G and Loftus E F (1979). 'Incorporating new information into memory', *American Journal of Psychology* 92(3), 413-425.

Coleman, L.(1989). 'Learning from the McMartin hoax', *Issues in Child Abuse Accusations*, 1 (2), 68-71.

Congreve William (1697). *The Morning Bride*, III, viii.

Constantine, Larry; Martinson, Floyd (1980). *Children and sex: new findings, new perspectives*, Little, Brown and Co, Boston.

Council on Scientific Affairs, American Medical Association (April 1985). 'Scientific status of refreshing recollection by the use of hypnosis', *Journal of American Medical Association*, 53(13) 1918-1923.

Crewdson John (1988). *By silence betrayed: sexual abuse of children in America*, Little, Brown and Co, Boston.

Cullen Michael, Minister of Social Welfare (17 Nov 1988). 'No "perfect solution" to protect children from abuse', *Key note address to Conference of the New Zealand Council of Social Services*, Hamilton.

Dawes Robyn (1989).'Experience and validity of clinical judgement: the illusory correla tion', *Behavioural Sciences and the Law*, 7(4), 000-000.

Dawes R, Faust D, Meehl P (31 March 1989).'Clinical versus actuarial judgement', *Science* 243, 1668-1674.

Dawes Robyn (20 June 1992). 'Why believe that for which there is no good evidence?', *Paper presented at Convention of American Psychological Society*, San Diego.

Dawson Raymond (1986). 'Confucius', in *Founders of Faith*, Oxford University Press, Oxford.

de Jong, A (May 1985). 'The medical examination of sexual abuse in children', *Hospital and Community Psychiatry*, 36 (5), 510-12.

Dent H (1991). 'Experimental studies of interviewing child witnesses', In J Doris (Ed) *The suggestibility of children's recollections: implications for eyewitness testimony*, American Psychological Association, Washington DC, 138-46.

Dent H (1982). 'The effects of interviewing strategies on the results of interviews with child witnesses', in Trankell A (Ed) *Reconstructing the Past* Deventer, The Netherlands, 279-98.

Dodd D, Bradshaw J (1980). 'Leading questions and memory: pragmatic constraints', *Journal of Verbal Learning and Verbal Behaviour* 19, 695-704.

Doe J (1991). 'How could this happen? Coping with a false allegation of incest and rape', *Issues in Child Abuse Accusations*, 3 (3), 154-65.

Edwards Brian (May 1983). 'In his own write: a cup of cold sick', *Metro*, Auckland, 143, 133-4.

Emans S Jean, Goldstein D P (April 1980). 'The gynecologic examination of the prepubertal child with vulvovaginitis: use of the knee-chest position', *Pediatrics*, 65 (4), 758-60.

Engel George (1977). 'The need for a new medical model: a challenge for biomedicine', *Science* 196 (4286), 129-36.

Engel George (1988). 'How much longer must medicine's science be bound by a 17th century world view?' in K White *The task of medicine: a dialogue at Wickenburg*, Henry Kaiser Family Foundation, California.

Engels Frederick ((1969). *The condition of the working class in England*, Grafton Books, Glasgow.

Everson M, Boat B (Mar 1989). 'False allegations of sexual abuse by children and adolescents', *Journal of the American Academy of Child and Adolescent Psychiatry* 28(2) 230-35.

Faludi Susan (1991). *Backlash: the undeclared war against women*, Chatto and Windus, London.

Fielding, W J (1961). *Strange customs of love and marriage*, Souvenir Press.

Finkelhor D (Oct 1985). 'An overview of the current knowledge about sexual abuse' *Surgeon General's Conference on Violence*, Leesburg.

Finkelhor D, Williams L M, Burns N (1988). *Nursery sexual abuse in day care*, Sage

Publications, California.

Fischhoff B, Slovic P, Litchenstein S (1977). 'Knowing with certainty: the appropriateness of extreme confidence', *Journal of Experimental Psychology: Human Perception and Performance* 3(4), 552-564.

Flin R (1991). 'Commentary: a grand memory for forgetting', in J Doris (Ed) *The suggestibility of children's recollections: implications for eyewitness testimony*, American Psychological Association, Washington DC, 21-3.

Foley M, Johnson M (1985). 'Confusions between memories for performed and imagined actions: a developmental comparison', *Child Development* 56,1145-55.

Ford, Cellan; Beach, Frank (1951). *Patterns of sexual behaviou*', Harper and Row, New York.

Foucault Michel (1976). *The history of sexuality*, Penguin Books.

Foucault Michel (1972). *Power/knowledge*, Pantheon Books.

Fox Matthew (1979). *A spirituality named compassion*, Harper and Row, San Franscisco.

Fox Matthew (1981). *Whee! we, wee all the way home: a guide to sensual, prophetic spirituality*, Bear and Co, New Mexico.

Fox Matthew (1983). *Original blessing*, Bear and Co Inc, New Mexico.

Franklin, Bob (1986). *The rights of children*, Basil Blackwell Ltd, Oxford

Freeman N V (31 October 1987). 'Letter to editor - child sexual abuse', *the Lancet*, 1017.

Fundudis T (May 1989). 'Children's memory and the assessment of possible child sex abuse', *Journal of Child Psychology and Psychiatry and Allied Disciplines* 30(3) 337-46.

Furman L, Walden T (1990). Effect of script knowledge on preschool children's communicative interactions', *Developmental Psychology* 26, 227-33.

Gamby J (1973). 'Father-daughter incest and the courts', *New Zealand Law Journal* 294-301.

Gardner R A (1991). *Sex abuse hysteria: Salem witch trials revisited*. Creative Therapeutics, New Jersey.

Gardner, Richard (1992). 'Belated realization of child sex abuse by an adult', *Issues in Child Abuse Accusations*, 4 (4), 177-95.

Gardner, Richard (1992). 'Leading stimuli, leading gestures and leading questions', *Issues in Child Abuse Accusations* 4(3), 144-55.

Gibran Kahlil ((1926). *The prophet*, William Heinmann Ltd.

Green A H (1986). 'True and false allegations of sexual abuse in child custody disputes', *Journal American Academy Child Psychiatry* 25:449-56.

Greene E, Flynn M, Loftus E (1982). 'Inducing resistance to misleading information', *Journal of Verbal Learning and Verbal Behaviour* 21, 207-19.

Greer Germaine (1970). *The Female Eunuch*, Granada Publishing, London.

Grutzner Anna (3 November 1992). 'Exclusive sex claims...pack of lies!', *Woman's Day*, 12-13.

Havelock Ellis (1936). *Studies in the psychology of sex, Volume 1*, Random House, New

York.
Hechler David (1988). *The Battle and the Backlash: the child sexual abuse law'* D C Heath and Co, United States.
Heger A (1985). *Child sexual abuse: a medical view,* United Way Inc, Los Angeles 2-3.
Herbert C (Aug 1985). 'The sexually abused child: the hidden victim', *Diagnosis,* 18-27
Herman Stephen (June 1992). 'Sexual abuse allegations in child custody cases: the role of the paediatrician', *Clinical Pediatrics,* 31 (6), 375.
Herr P (1986).'Consequences of priming: judgement and behaviour', *Journal of Person ality and Social Psychology* 51: 1106-15.
Hobbs C, Wynne J (1986). 'Buggery in childhood', *The Lancet,* ii, 792-6.
Hobbs, C; Wynne J. (10 Oct 1987). 'Child sexual abuse: an increasing rate of diagnosis', *The Lancet* 2 (8563), 837-41.
Hobbs C, Wynne J (1989). 'Sexual abuse of English boys and girls: the importance of anal examination', *Child Abuse and Neglect,* 13, 195-210.
Hollin C H, Clifford B R (1983). 'Eye witness testimony: the effects of discussion on recall accuracy and agreement', *Journal of Applied Social Psychology* 13(3) 234-44.
Hollingsworth, Jan (1986). *Unspeakable acts,* Congdon and Weed, New York.
Howitt, Dennis (1992). *Child abuse errors: when good intentions go wrong,* Harvester Wheatsheaf, Hamel Hempstead.
Hughes M, Grieve R (1983). 'On asking children bizarre questions', in Donaldson M, Grieve R, Pratt C (eds) *Early childhood development and education: readings in psychology,* 1983 New York: the Guilford Press, 105-144.
Hughes Roy (19 Nov 1983). 'A moral dilemma', *the Christchurch Shopping Guide.*
James D (1988). 'Child abuse after Cleveland', *The Lancet* 2: 398.
James K (1986). 'Priming and social categorizational factors: impact on awareness of emergency situations', *Personality and Social Psychology Bulletin* 12: 462-7.
Jenny Carole, Huhns Mary, Arakawa Fukiho. *The presence of hymens in newborn female infants,* Harbourview Medical Center, Seattle (paper from author).
Jones D, McGraw J (1987). 'Reliable and fictitious accounts of sexual abuse of children', *Journal of Interpersonal Violence,* 2, 27-45.
Jones, E.D.; McCurdy K. (1992). 'The links between types of maltreatment and demographical characteristics of children', *Child Abuse and Neglect,* 16, 201-15.
Jones, J. (Feb 1982). 'Sexual abuse of children: current concepts', *American Journal of Diseases of Children,* 136, 142-6.
Kasl Charlotte (April 1986). 'The role of spirituality in recovery from sexual assault', *Abstracts, International Congress on Rape,* Israel.
Kassin S, Ellsworth P, Smith V (1989). 'The "general acceptance" of psychological research on eyewitness testimony', *American Psychologist* 44(8), 1089-98.
Kean H B (31 Oct 1987). 'Letter to the Editor, Child sexual abuse', *the Lancet,* 1018.
Kelly L (Jan 1988). 'What's in a name?: defining child sexual abuse', *Feminist Review* 28:

65-73.

Kempe C H, Kempe R S (1978). *Child Abuse*, Fontana Open Books.

Kiefer Louis (1989). 'Defence considerations in the child as witness in allegations of sexual abuse Part II. The child witness: legal competency', *Issues in Child Abuse Accusations* 1 (2), 48-57.

Kilpatrick, Allie (May 1986). 'Some correlates of women's childhood sexual experiences: a retrospective study', *The Journal of Sex Research*, 22 (2), 221-42.

Kinsey A et al (1948). *Sexual behaviour in the human male*, Saunders, Philadelphia.

Kinsey A et al (1953). *Sexual behaviour in the human female*, Saunders, Philadelphia.

Kiser, L J, Heston J, Millsap P A, Pruitt D B (Sept 1991). 'Physical and sexual abuse in childhood: relationship with post-traumatic stress disorder', *Journal of American Academy of Child and Adolescent Psychiatry*, 30 (5), 776-83.

Klajner-Diamond H, Wehrspann W, Steinhauer P (Oct 1987).'Assessing the credibility of young children's allegations of sexual abuse: clinical issues', *Canadian Journal of Psychiatry* 32(7) 610-14.

Kobasigawa A (1974). 'Utilisation of retrieval cues by children in recall', *Child Development* 127-34.

Kolata Gina (20 Dec 1991). 'Critic of DNA tests tells of pressure to withdraw', *New York Times*.

Krentz Johnston M S (1979). 'The sexually mistreated child: diagnostic evaluation', *Child Abuse and Neglect*, 3, 943-51.

Krivacska James (1989). 'Primary prevention of child sexual abuse: alternative, non-child directed approaches', *Issues in Child Abuse Accusations*, 1 (4), 1-9.

Krivacska James (9 June 1991). 'Child sexual abuse prevention programs: the prevention of childhood sexuality?', page presented at the *Society for the Scientific Study of Sex Seventh Midcontinent Annual Conference Plenary Session*.

Krivacska James (1991). 'Sexual Abuse prevention programs: can they cause false allegations?', *Issues in Child Abuse Accusations*, 3 (1), 1-6.

Krugman R D (July 1986). 'Recognition of sexual abuse in young children', *Pediatrics in Review*, 8 (10, 25-27.

La Fontaine, Jean (1990). *Child sexual abuse*, Polity Press, England.

Langford R E (1990). *Book review: Kinsey, Sex and Fraud: the indoctrination of a people. An investigation into the human sexuality research of Kinsey, Pomeroy, Martin and Gebhard*, edited by J Muir and J Court.

Langwirth J (Oct 1987). 'Children as witnesses in Child sexual abuse trials', *Paediatrics* 80(4) 585-9.

Lawton Margaret, Goodyear Felicity, Stringer Peta (1987). *Sexual assault examinations - a guide for medical practitioners*, DSIR, Wellington.

Lechky O (15 Oct 1991). 'Incest can have devastating emotional and physical consequences, women physicians told', *Canadian Medical Association Journal* 145(8)

1020, 1022-25.

Leitenberg H, Greenwald E, Tarran J (1989). 'The relationship between sexual activity among children during preadolescence and/or early adolescence and sexual behaviour and sexual adjustment in young adulthood', *Archives of Sexual Behaviour*, 18(4) 299-313.

Lepore, S (1991). 'Child witness: cognitive and social factors related to memory and testimony', *Issues in Child Abuse Accusations* 3(2) 65-89.

Lewontin R, Hartl Daniel (20 Dec 1991). 'Population genetics in forensic DNA typing', *Science* 254, 1745-50.

Li C, West D, Woodhouse T (1990). *Children's sexual encounters with adults*, Duckworth, London.

Lindberg M (1991).'An interactive approach to assessing the suggestibility and testimony of eyewitnesses', in J Doris (ed) *The suggestibility of children's recollections: implications for eyewitness testimony*, American Psychological Association, Washington DC, 47-55.

Lindsay D (1990). 'Misleading suggestions can impair eyewitnesses' ability to remember event details', *Journal of Experimental Psychology: Learning, Memory and Cognition* 16(6) 1077-83.

Lipton J (1977).'On the psychology of eyewitness testimony', *Journal of Applied Psychology* 62 90-5.

Loftus, Elizabeth (1975). 'Leading questions and the eyewitness report' *Cognitive Psychology* 7(40), 560-72.

Loftus Elizabeth (Feb 1984). 'Eyewitnesses: essential but unreliable', Psychology Today 22-6.

Loftus E, Burns T (1982). 'Mental shock can produce retrograde amnesia', *Memory and Cognition* 10(4), 318-23.

Loftus E, Burns H, Miller D (1978). 'Semantic integration of verbal information into a visual memory', *Journal of Experimental Psychology: Human Learning and Memory* 4 (1), 19-31.

Loftus, E, Davies G (1984). 'Distortions in the memories of children', *Journal of Social Issues* 40(2), 51-67.

Loftus E, Korf K, Schooler J (1989). 'Misguided memories: sincere distortion of reality', in Yuille J (ed), *Credibility Assessment*, Kluwer Academic Publishers.

Loftus E, Schooler J, Wagenaar W (1985). 'The fate of memory: comment on McCloskey and Zaragoza', *Journal of Experimental Psychology: General* 114(3), 375-80.

MacFarlane Kee (1986). *Sexual abuse of young children*, The Gailford Press, California.

MacLeod M and Saraga E (Jan 1988). 'Challenging orthodoxy towards a feminist theory and practice', *Feminist Review*, 28 16-55.

MacWhinney B, Keenan J, Reinke P (1982). 'The role of arousal in memory for conversation', *Memory and Cognition*, 10 (4) 308-17.

Malinowski, B (1929). *The sexual life of savages*, Routledge and Sons, England.
Mandel Ernest (1979). *Introduction to Marxism*, Ink Links Ltd, London.
Mandler J, Johnson N (1977). 'Remembrance of things passed: story structure and recall', *Cognitive Psychology* 9:111-51.
Margo G M, McLees E M (1991). 'Further evidence for the significance of a childhood abuse history in psychiatric inpatients', *Comprehensive Psychiatry*, 32 (4), 362-6.
Marshall D, Suggs R (Eds) (1971). *Human sexual behaviour: variations in the ethnographic spectrum*, Basic Books, New York.
Masters W, Johnson V (1970). *Human Sexual Inadequacy*, Little, Brown and Co, Boston.
Max Lesley (1990). *Children: endangered species?*, Penguin Books, Auckland.
McCann John, Voris Joan, Simon Mary, Wells Robert (1989). 'Perianal findings in prepubertal children selected for nonabuse: a descriptive study', *Child Abuse and Neglect*, 13, 179-193.
McCann John, Voris Joan, Simon Mary (Feb 1992). 'Genital injuries resulting from sexual abuse: a longitudinal study', *Pediatrics*, 89 (2), 307-17.
McCarthy, Barry (1990). 'A cognitive-behavioural approach to the treatment of incestuous families', in *Violence hits home: comprehensive treatment approaches to domestic violence* edited by Stith, Williams and Rosen, Springer Publishing Company, New York.
McCloskey M, Zaragoza M (1985). 'Postevent information and memory: reply to Loftus, Schooler and Wagenaar', *Journal of Experimental Psychology: General* 114(3), 381-7.
McWhinney Ian (1989). *Family Practice*, Oxford University Press.
Medlicott R (1967). 'Parent-child incest', *Australian and New Zealand Journal of Psychiatry* 1, 180-7.
Medlicott R (1979). 'Parent-child incest', in *Deviant behaviour New Zealand studies* edited by W Black and A Taylor, Heinmann Educational Books.
Millett Kate (1969). *Sexual Politics*, Rupert Hart-Davis, London.
Millett Kate (1991). 'Sexual revolution and the liberation of children', An interview with Kate Millett by Mark Blasius, *Paidika*.
Money John (June 1991). 'Epidemic antisexualism: from onanism to satanism', *Opening Plenary Speech for 10th World Congress of Sexology*, Amsterdam.
Money John (Spring 1991). 'From sin to science: tolerance of homosexuality', *Free Inquiry*, 2(2), 32-6.
Money John (Feb/Mar 1991). 'Sexology and/or sexosophy: the split between sexual researchers and reformers in history and practice', *Siecus Report*, 19(3), 1-4.
Money, John; Prakasam, K Swayam; Joshi, Ventkat N (1991). 'Transcultural developmental sexology: genital greeting versus child molestation', *Issues In Child Abuse Accusations*, 3 (4), 215-6.
Moore Jean (1985). *The ABC of child abuse work*, Gower Publishing Company Ltd, England.

Mrazek P (Jan 1980). 'Sexual abuse of children', *Journal of Child Psychology and Psychiatry* 21(1) 91-5.

Mullen, Paul (20 July 1990). 'The consequences of child sexual abuse', *British Medical Journal*, 303 (67950, 144-5.

Mullen P, Romans-Clarkson S, Walton V, Herbison G (16 Apr 1988). 'Impact of Sexual and Physical Abuse on Women's Mental Health', *The Lancet* 841-5.

Mullen P, Anderson J, Roman-Clarkson S, Martin J (1991). *Otago women's health survey child abuse study*, unpublished.

Muram, D (Mar 1992). 'Child sexual abuse', *Pediatric and Adolescent Gynecology*, 19 (1), 193-207.

Myles-Worsley M, Comer C, Dodd D (1986). 'Children's preschool script reconstruction: reliance on general knowledge as memory fades', *Developmental Psychology* 22(1), 22-30.

Nelson Joan (Nov 1986). 'Incest: self-report findings from a nonclinical sample', *Journal of Sex Research* 22 (4) 463-77.

Nelson, Joan (1989). 'Intergenerational sexual contact: a continuum model of participants and experiences', *Journal of Sex Education and Therapy* 15 (1), 3-12.

O'Carroll, Tom (1980). *Paedophilia: the radical case*, Alyson publications, Boston.

O'Connell D, Shor R, Orne M (Dec 1970).'Hypnotic age regression: an empirical and methodological analysis', *Journal of Abnormal Psychology Monograph*, 76(3) Part 2.

Olafson Erna, Corwin David, Summit Roland (1993). 'Modern history of child sexual abuse awareness: cycles of discovery and suppression', *Child Abuse and Neglect*, 17, 7-24.

Orne M (April 1951). 'The mechanisms of hypnotic age regression: an experimental study', *Journal of Abnormal and Social Psychology*, 46 (2), 213-25.

Orne M (1984). 'Hypnosis "useful in medicine, dangerous in court"', *US News and World Report*, Washington.

Orne M, Whitehouse W, Dinges D, Orne E (1988). 'Reconstructing memory through hypnosis: forensic and clinical implications', in H Pettinani (ed) *Hypnosis and Memory*, Guilford Press, New York.

Ornstein P (1991). 'Commentary: putting interviewing in context', in J Doris (ed) *The suggestibility of children's recollections: implications for eyewitness testimony* American Psychological Association, Washington DC, 147-52 .

Orwell George (1945). *Animal farm*, Great Britain.

Oshima-Takane Y (1988). 'Children learn from speech not addressed to them: the case of personal pronouns', *Journal of Child Language* 15, 95-108.

Paglia Camille (1991). *Sexual Personae: art and decadence from Nefertiti to Emily Dickinson*, Vintage books New York.

Paradise Jan, Rostain Anthony, Nathanson Madelaine (6 June 1988). 'Substantiation of sexual abuse charges when parents dispute custody or visitation', *Pediatrics*, 81 (6),

835-9.

Parton, Nigel (1985). *The politics of child abuse*, MacMillan Education Ltd, London.

Peck Scott (1978). *A road less travelled: a new psychology of love, traditional values and spiritual growth*, Rider, London.

Perlmutter M, Ricks M (1979). 'Recall in preschool children', *Journal of Experimental Child Psychology* 27: 423-6.

Peters D (1991). 'The influence of stress and arousal on the child witness', in J Doris (ed) *The suggestibility of children's recollections: implications for eyewitness testimony*, American Psychological Association, Washington DC, 60-76.

Petersen Hollis (1991). 'How to get removed from a Central Registry', *Issues in Child Abuse Accusations*, 3 (4), 232-3.

Pfohl S (Spring/Summer 1979). 'Deciding on dangerousness: predictions of violence as social control', *Crime and Social Justice* 28-40.

Plunkett A, Oates R (Jul 1990). 'Methodological considerations in research in child sexual abuse', *Paediatric and Perinatal Epidemiology* 4(3) 351-60.

Pokorny Susan, Pokorny William, Kramer Wayne (1992). 'Acute genital injury in the prepubetal girl', *American Journal of Obstetrics and Gynecology*, 166, 1461-6.

Pribor E.F. and Dinwiddie S.H. (Jan 1992). 'Psychiatric correlates of incest in childhood', *American Journal of Psychiatry*, 149 (1), 52-6.

Pride, Mary (1986). *The Child Abuse Industry*, Crossway Books, Illinois.

Rabinowitz Dorothy (May 1990). 'From the mouths of babes to a jail cell. Child abuse and the abuse of justice: a case study', *Harpers Magazine*, 52-63.

Rand Deidre Conway (1989). 'Munchausen syndrome by proxy as a possible factor when abuse is falsely alleged', *Issues in Child Abuse Accusations*, 1 (4), 32-4.

Rand Deidre Conway (1990). 'Munchausen syndrome by proxy: integration of classic and contemporary types', *Issues in Child Abuse Accusations*, 2 (2), 83-9.

Raphael K, Cloitre M, Dohrenwend B (1991). 'Problems of recall and misclassification with checklist methods of measuring stressful life events', *Health psychology* 10(1), 62-74.

Reed Christopher (27 May 1992). 'Town law says looks must not count', *The Age*, 7.

Rich C, Herman J, Perry C (Oct 1989). 'Letters to the Editor; Verifying patients' Reports of Childhood Abuse', *American Journal of Psychiatry* 146(10) 1358-9.

Richardson J T, Best J, Bromley D G (1991). *The satanism scare*, Aldine de Gruyter, New York.

Roberts Leslie 20 Dec 1991. 'Fight erupts over DNA fingerprinting', *Science*, 254, 1721-3.

Rogers, M L (1990). 'Coping with alleged false sexual molestation: examination and statement analysis procedures', *Issues in Child Abuse Accusations* 2 (2), 57-68.

Rogers, M L (20 June 1992). 'Evaluating adult litigants who allege injuries from child sexual abuse: clinical assessment methods for traumatic memories', Presented at *symposium, Fourth Annual Meeting of American Psychological Society*, California.

Rosenfeld AA, Nadelson CC, Krieger M (1979). 'Fantasy and reality in patients' reports of incest', *Journal Clinical Psychiatry* 40:159-64.

Rosenfeld M, Bailey R, Siegel B, Bailey G (1986). 'Determining incestuous contact between parent and child: frequency of children touching parents' genitals in a nonclinical population', *Journal of American Academy of Psychiatry* 25(4) 481-4.

Ross Colin, Norton G Ron (Oct 1989). 'Effects of hypnosis on the features of multiple personality disorder', *American Journal of Clinical Hypnosis*, 32 (2), 99-106.

Ross C, Norton G (Oct 1989). 'The effects of hypnosis on the features of multiple personality disorder', *American Journal of Clinical Hypnosis* 32(2) 99-106.

Ross Karol, Blush Gordon (1990). 'Sexual abuse validity discriminators in the divorced or divorcing family', *Issues in Child Abuse Accusations*, 2 (1), 1-6.

Rossen B (1989). 'Mass hysteria in Oude Pekela', *Issues in Child Abuse Accusations*, 1 (1), 49-51.

Royal College of Physicians of London (1991). *Physical signs of sexual abuse in children*, Cathedral Press Ltd, Salisbury, Wilts.

Rubin D (Sept 1985). 'The subtle deceiver: recalling our past', *Psychology today* 39-46.

Rush Florence (1980). *The best-kept secret: sexual abuse of children*, TAB Books, Blue Ridge Books, PA.

Russell D (1983). 'The incidence and prevalence of intrafamilial sexual abuse of female children', *Child Abuse and Neglect*, 7 (2), 133-76.

Sanford Linda (1990). *Strong at the broken places: overcoming the trauma of childhood abuse*, Random House, New York.

Saphira Miriam ((1985). *The sexual abuse of children*, Papers Inc, Auckland.

Saphira Miriam ((1987). *For your child's sake: understanding sexual abuse*, Reed Methuen, Auckland.

Saunders E (1988). 'A comparative study of attitudes toward child sexual abuse among social work and judicial system professionals', *Child Abuse and Neglect* 12(1) 83-90.

Saywitz K (1897). 'Children's testimony: age-related patterns of memory errors', in Ceci S, Toglia M, Ross D (eds) *Children's Eyewitness Memory*, New York, Springer-Verlag, 36-52.

Schaeff Anne Wilson (1992). *Beyond therapy, beyond science: a new model for healing the whole person*, Harper, San Francisco.

Schechter and Roberge, (1976). Area Health Boards Policy.

Schetky D, Green A H (1987). *Child Sexual Abuse*, Brunner/Mazel, New York.

Schooler J, Gerhard D, Loftus E (1986). 'Qualities of the unreal', *Journal of Experimental Psychology: Learning, Memory and Cognition* 12(2), 171-81.

Schuijer Jan, Rossen Benjamin (1992). 'The trade in child pornography', *Issues in Child Abuse Accusations*, 4 (20, 55-107).

Schultz, Leroy G (1982). 'Child sexual abuse in historical perspective', *Journal of Social*

Work and Human Sexuality, 1 (1-2), 21-35.

Schultz Leroy (1990). 'Self-help groups for the erroneously charged: a proposed model', *Issues in Child Abuse Accusations,* 2 (2), 109-15.

Schultz L, Jones P (1983). 'Sexual abuse of children: issues for social service and health professionals', *Child Welfare,* 62(2):99-108.

Schwartz, M (1982).'Repetition and the rated true value of statements', *American Journal of Psychology* 95(3), 393-407.

Scott K D (1992). 'Childhood sexual abuse: impact on a community's mental status', *Child Abuse and Neglect,* 16, 285-95.

Sheridan Robert (1990). 'The false child molestation outbreak of the 1980s: an explanation of the cases arising in the divorce context', *Issues in Child Abuse Accusations,* 2 (3), 146-51.

Sgroi S (1982). H*andbook of clinical intervention in child sexual abus*', Lexington Books, Lexington, MA.

Siegel Bernie (1986). *Love, medicine and miracles,* Arrow Books, London.

Siegel Richard; Strassfeld Michael; Strassfeld Sharon (1973). *The Jewish catalog,* The Jewish Publication Society of America, Philadelphia.

Slaby R; Quarfoth G (1980). 'Effects of television on the developing child', in *Advances in behavioural paediatrics* edited by B Camp, JAI Press, Greenwich, 1, 225-66.

Slackman E, Nelson K (1984). 'Acquisition of an unfamiliar script in story form by young children', *Child Development* 55, 329-40.

Spanos Nicholas, Weekes John, Bertrand Lorne (1985). 'Multiple personality: a social psychological perspective', *Journal of Abnormal Psychology,* 94 (3), 362-76.

Spiegel D (June 1989). 'Hypnosis in the treatment of victims of sexual abuse', *Psychiatric Clinics of North America* 12(2) 295-305.

Stanley Lawrence (1989). 'The child porn myth', *Cardozo Arts and Entertainment Law Journal,* 7, 2, 295-358.

Starhawk (1987). *Truth or dare: encounters with power, authority and mystery,* Harper, San Francisco.

Stayton Rowe (1991). 'Plaintiff's brief regarding the constitutionality of Central Registry', *Issues in Child Abuse Accusations,* 3 (4), 234-9.

Stecher G (7 Feb 1980). 'Facing the problem of the sexually abused child', *New England Journal of Medicine,* 302 (6), 348-9.

Steele G, Henderson S, Duncan-Jones P (1980). 'The reliability of reporting adverse experiences', *Psychological Medicine,* 10, 301-306.

Stirling Pamela (6 Feb 1993). 'Breaking the silence', *Listener,* 18-19.

Summit Roland (1983). 'The child abuse accommodation syndrome', *Child Abuse and Neglect,* 7, 177-93.

Summit R C. *Helping the physician entertain the diagnosis of child sexual abuse,* National Committee for the Prevention of Child Abuse.

Sunderland R (31 Oct 1987). 'Letters to the Editor - child sexual abuse, *the Lancet*, 1018.

Toffler, Alvin (1990). *Powershift*, Bantam books, New York.

Turvill Phyllis (Aug 1986). 'Child sexual abuse: how to cope and when to act', *Modern Medicine*, 14-15.

Underwager Ralph (1990). 'Affidavit of Ralph Underwager, Ph.D', *Issues in Child Abuse Accusations* 2 (1), 36-46.

Underwager Ralph, Wakefield Hollida (1990). *The real world of child interrogations*, Charles Thomas Publisher.

Underwager Ralph, Wakefield Hollida (1991). 'Cur alii, prae aliis? (why some, not others?)', *Issues in Child Abuse Accusations* 3(3) 178-93.

Underwager Ralph, Wakefield Hollida (1991). 'Central registry: protection or oppression?', *Issues in Child Abuse Accusations*, 3 (4), 221-7.

Vandierendonck A, van Damme R (1988). 'Schema anticipation in recall: memory process or report strategy?', *Psychological Research* 50, 116-22.

Victor Jeffrey S (1991). 'The satanic cult scare and allegations of ritual child abuse', *Issues in Child Abuse Accusations* 3 (3), 135-143.

von Dadelszen J (Feb/Mar 1988). 'Sexual abuse study: an examination of the histories of sexual abuse among girls currently in the care of the Department of Social Welfare - a summary report', *Mental Health News* 19-20.

Wakefield Hollida, Underwager Ralph (1988). *Accusations of child sexual abuse*, Charles Thomas Publisher, Springfield, Illinois.

Wakefield Hollida, Underwager Ralph (1989). 'Interrogation of children', *Issues in Child Abuse Accusations* 1 (1), 14-28.

Wakefield Hollida, Underwager Ralph (1989). 'Evaluating the child witness in sexual abuse cases: interview or inquisition?', *American Journal of Forensic Psychology* 7(3) 43-69.

Wakefield, Hollida, Underwager Ralph (1989). 'Manipulating the child sexual abuse system', *Issues in Child Abuse Accusations*, 1 (2), 58-67.

Wakefield Hollida, Underwager Ralph (1990). 'Personality characteristics of parents making false accusations of sexual abuse in custody disputes', *Issues in Child Abuse Accusations* 2(3) 121-36.

Wakefield Hollida, Underwager Ralph (1991). 'Sexual abuse allegations in divorce and custody disputes', *Behavioural Sciences and the Law*, 9, 451-68.

Wakefield Hollida, Underwager Ralph (1991). 'Sexual abuse allegations in divorce and custody disputes'. *Behavioural Sciences and the Law* 9 451-68.

Wakefield Hollida, Underwager Ralph (1991). 'Assessing credibility of children's testimony in cases of ritual sexual abuse allegations', *Issues in Child Abuse Accusations*, 4 (1), 32-44.

Watkins B, Bentovim A (1992). 'The sexual abuse of male children and adolescents: a review of current literature', *Journal of Child Psychiatry and Psychiatry*, 33 (1), 197-

248.

Warren-Leubecker A (1991). 'The influence of stress and arousal on the child witness', in J Doris (ed) *The suggestibility of children's recollections: implications for eyewitness testimony*, American Psychological Association, Washington DC, 60-76.

Weeks, Jeffrey (1987). 'Questions in identity', in *The cultural construction of sexuality*, by Caplan (ed), Tavistock, London.

Weeks, Jeffrey (1981). *Sex, politics and society*, Longman, England.

Wehrspann W, Steinhauer P, Klajner-Diamond H (Oct 1987). 'Criteria and methodology for assessing credibility of sexual abuse allegation', *Canadian Journal of Psychiatry* 32(7) 615-23.

Wells G L (1982). 'Attribution and reconstructive memory', *Journal of Experimental Social Psychology* 18, 447-63.

West, D J (Nov 1988). 'Incest in childhood and adolescence: long-term effects and therapy', *British Journal of Hospital Medicine*, 40, 352-60.

Whalen Jeff (1991). 'Florida abuse registry loses in Federal Court', *Issues in Child Abuse Accusations*, 3 (4), 228-31.

Whitman B, Munkel W (July 1991). 'Multiple Personality Disorder: A Risk Indicator, Diagnostic Marker and Psychiatric Outcome for Severe Child Abuse', *Clinical Paediatrics* 30(7) 422-8.

Widom Cathy Spatz (1989). 'Does violence beget violence? A critical examination of the literature', *Psychological Bulletin*, 106 (1), 3-28.

Wilson J; Herrstein R (1985). *Crime and human nature*, Simon and Schuster, New York.

Wilson Paul (April 1986). 'False complaints by children of sexual abuse', *Legal Service Bulletin*, 79-83.

Winefield H, McGregor S Aug 1987). 'Child sexual abuse cases: facilitating their detection and reporting by General Practitioners', *Australian Journal of Social Issues* 22(3) 27-36.

Wong Donna (Sept/Oct 1987). 'False allegations of child abuse: the other side of the tragedy', *Pediatric Nursing*, 13 (5), 329-32.

Woodling B, Kossoris P (May 1981). 'Sexual misuse: rape, molestation and incest', *Pediatric Clinics of North America*, 28 (2).

Woodling Bruce, Heger Astrid (1986). 'The use of the colposcope in the diagnosis of sexual abuse in the pediatric age group', *Child Abuse and Neglect*, 10, 111-14.

Woods Mary Helen (July 1988). 'Child abuse - fact and fantasy', *Family*, 8-9.

Wurtele S K, Kaplan G M, Keairnes M. (1990). 'Childhood sexual abuse amongst chronic pain patients', *Clinical Journal of Pain*, 6, 110-13.

Yates A, Musty T (Aug 1988). 'Preschool children's erroneous allegations of sexual molestation', *American Journal of Psychiatry* 145(8) 989-92.

Yates A (April 1987). 'Should children testify in cases of sexual abuse?', *American Journal of Psychiatry* 144(4) 476-80.

Zaragoza M (1991). 'Preschool children's susceptibility to memory impairment', in J Doris (ed) *The suggestibility of children's recollections: implications for eyewitness testimony*, (pp 27-39), American Psychological Association, Washington DC, 27-39.

Zeitlin H (10 Oct 1987). 'Investigation of the sexually abused child', *the Lancet* 2(8563) 842-5.

Zelas K (Jan 1987). 'Incest: a problem of major proportions', *Patient Management* 33-34.

Name index

Accident Compensation Commission (ACC) 105-6
American Medical Association 51, 57
Anderson, W. 16, 17, 127
Archer, E. 37
Aries, P. 65, 132
Aristotle 35
Augustine, St. 132

Bacchmann, G. 54, 62
Bass, E. 35, 50, 131, 138
Baurrmann, M. 69
Beach, F. 66
Bejin, A. 132
Ben-Yehuda, N. 24, 25
Bentovim, A. 58, 62
Bernard, V. 117
Besharov, D. 107, 108
Birnbaum, J. 129
Blush, G. 97
Bly, R. 136
Boat, B. 40, 102
Bonanno, G. 51
Bradshaw, J. 43
Braga, L. and J. 79
Brant, R. 59
Bravos, Z. 23
Brehmer, B. 51
Bresee, P. 97
Brody, H. 18, 134
Brongersma, E. 64, 71
Bruck, M. 44
Buddha 16, 131
Burns, T. 42, 52

Campbell, B. 118, 122
Cantwell, H. 115
Caplan, P. 20

Ceci, S. 42, 44
Chakraborty, R. 123
Clifford, B. 45
Cole, W. 42
Coleman, L. 46, 77, 78, 79
Confucius 131
Congreve, W. 96
Constantine, L. 67-9, 72-3
Copernicius 16
Corwin, D. 125, 126
Council on Scientific Affairs 51
Crewdson, J. 35, 77
Cullen, M. 109

Damme, R. 44, 47
Dante 64
Davis, L. 35, 50, 131, 138
Dawes, R. 43, 46, 51, 52
Dawson, R. 131
Densen-Gerber, J. 92
Dent, H. 47
Descartes, R. 17
Dinwiddie, S. 60
Disraeli, B. 54
Dodd, D. 43
Doe, J. 51

Edwards, B. 129
Elwin, V. 69
Engel, G. 134
Engels, F. 128
Euripides 40
Everson, M. 40, 102

Faludi, S. 125
Fielding, W. 65
Finkelhor, D. 35, 57, 71, 78, 119
Fischhoff, B. 43

Flinn, R. 44
Foley, M. 45
Ford, C. 66
Foucault, M. 17, 19, 22
Fox, M. 20, 132
Franklin, B. 72
Freeman, N. 117
Freud, S. 45, 68
Fundudis, T. 47
Furman, L. 47

Galileo 16
Gardner, R. 44, 61, 125
Gibran, K. 127, 133, 136
Goodyear, F. 115
Graham, M. 22
Grieve, R. 43
Grutzner, A. 105

Hammurabi 38
Hartl, D. 123
Havelock E. 19
Hechler, D. 112, 126
Heger, A. 57, 116
HELP Sexual Assault Centre 6-8, 57, 110
Henry IV 65
Herbert, C. 62
Herman, S. 97
Heroard 65
Herr, P. 47
Herrstein, R. 130
Higgs, M. 117, 122
Hillel 132
Hippocrates 10, 38
Hitler, A. 23
Hobbs, C. 117
Hollin, C. 45
Hollingsworth, J. 79
Howitt, D. 22, 108, 125

Hughes, M. 43
Hughes, R. 111

Ives, R. 72

James, K. 47
Jesus 132
Johnson, M. 45
Johnson, V. 30, 68
Jones, D. 97
Jones, P. 69

Kasl, C. 133
Kassin, S. 53
Kean, B. 117
Kellogg, J. 22
Kelly, L. 57, 59
Kempe, H. 34, 58
Kidd, K. 123
Kiefer, L. 40
Kilpatrick, A. 69
Kinsey, A. 30, 68
Kiser, L. 60
Klajner-Diamond, H. 40
Kobasigawa, A. 40
Kolata, G. 123
Korf, K. 42, 46
Kossoris, P. 56
Krivacska, J. 121, 122
Krugman, R. 58

la Fontaine, J. 118, 122
Landwirth, J. 73
Langford, r. 68
Lawton, M. 115
Lecky, O. 62
Leitenberg, H. 69
Lewontin, R. 123
Li, C. 69
Lindberg, M. 43

Lindsay, D. 42
Lipton, J. 42
Lloyd, R. 92
Loftus, E. 42-3, 46, 47, 52
Louis XIII 65

MacFarlane, K. 35, 77, 97, 107
MacLeod, M. 38
Malinowski, B. 67
Malthus, T. 21
Mandel, E. 128
Margo, G. 60
Marshall, D 68
Martinson, F. 67, 68, 69
Masters, W. 30, 68
Mather, I. 107
Max, L. 111
McCann, J. 115, 117
McCarthy, Senator 25
McCloskey, M. 43
McGraw, J. 97
McIlveena, T. 86
McLees, E. 60
Meadows, R. 114
Medlicott, R. 62, 103
Mental Health Foundation of New Zealand 35
Millett, K. 71
Money, J. 20 23, 29, 38, 45, 59, 67, 129
Moore, J. 35
Mrazek, P. 56
Mullens, P. 62, 73
Musty, T. 40
Myles-Worsley, M. 44

Nelson, J. 37, 70, 73
North American Man/Boy Association (NAMBA) 71
NSW Child Protection Council 57

O'Carroll, T. 71
O'Connell, T. 51
Olafson, E. 125, 126
Orne, M. 50, 51
Ornstein, P. 46, 47
Orwell, G. 128
Oshima-Takane, Y. 46
Ovid 135

Paedophile Information Exchange (PIE) 70
Paglia, C. 32, 125, 131
Parents Against INjustice (PAIN) 126
Parton, N. 65
Peck, S. 127, 133, 136
Peters, D. 52
Peterson, H. 124
Pfohl, S. 52
Plato 16
Pokorny, S. 115
Pope, A. 127
Pribor, E. 60
Pride, M. 46, 110, 111, 125

Quarforth, G. 130

Rabinowitz, D. 81
Rand, D. 114
Raphael, K. 52
Reed, C. 129
Rene Guyon Society 70
Richardson, J. 83, 113
Roberts, R. 116, 122
Rogers, M. 36, 50
Rosenfeld, A. 45, 60, 69
Ross, K. 97
Rossen, B. 84, 92, 93
Royal College of Physicians 115, 116, 117

Rubin, D. 51
Rush, F. 35, 92, 107
Russell, D. 35, 37

Sandfort, T. 35, 70
Saphira, M. 35, 62
Saraga, E. 38
Saunders, E. 55
Saywitz, K. 42
Schaef, A. 131, 132, 134
Schooler, J. 42, 43, 46
Schuijer, J. 92, 93
Schultz, L. 33, 64, 69, 126
Schwartz, M. 44
Scott, K. 60
Sexual Abuse Rehabilitation Therapy Centre (START) 116
Sgroi, S. 40
Sheridan, R. 97
Siegel, B. 127, 133
Siegel, R. 135
Slaby, R. 130
Slackman, E. 44
Society for the Prevention of Cruelty to Children 33
Spanos, N. 112
Stanley, L. 93, 94
Starhawk 133
Stecher, G. 61
Steele, G. 52
Stringer, P. 115
Summit, R. 34, 107, 111, 114, 119, 125, 126, 139
Sunderland, R. 117

Tissot, S. 22
Tisva, V 59
Toffler, A. 133
Turvill, P. 58

Underwager, R. 24, 33, 36, 46, 47, 58, 73, 77, 81, 83, 84, 97, 101, 115, 123, 125

van Mander, C. 64
Vandierendonck, A. 44, 47
Victims of Child Abuse Laws (VOCAL) 126
Victor, J. 45, 47, 86
von Dadzelszen, J. 59
von Munchausen, Baron 114

Wakefield, H. 24, 36, 46, 65, 73, 77, 83, 84, 97, 101, 115, 123, 125
Walden, T. 47
Warren-Leubecker, A. 41
Weeks, J. 19, 22, 24
Wells, G. 42
West, D. 68
Whalen, J. 110, 124
Widom, C. 130
Wilson, P. 102, 103
Wojt, J. 37
Wong, D. 46, 48, 54
Woodling, B. 56
Woods, M. 117
Wyatt, G. 117, 122
Wynne, J. 117

Yates, A. 40, 73
Zeitlin, H. 41, 73

Subject index

Accuracy
  of clinical judgements 51-2
  of memory 41, 43, 52
  under stress 52
Accident Compensation Commission (ACC) 105-6
AIDS 21, 28, 29
Alternative communities 86-91
Australia
  cases in 87, 102
  sexual abuse issues in 57, 126

Backlash movement 15, 41, 119, 125-6
Behavioural indicators 76, 140, 22-3
Belief systems 36, 62, 71, 127, 132
Beliefs, cycles in 22-4
Branch Davidians 91
Buddhism 16, 131

Centrepoint Community case 8-12, 87-91, 94, 104
Child daycare cases 76-82
Child pornography 92-5
Child sexual abuse
  definitions of 54-61
  diagnosis of 140
  history of 33-4
  prevalence of 37, 58-63
  prevention programs 36, 97, 120-22
Child Abuse Accommodation Syndrome 111-12
Childhood sexuality 64-74
  anthropological studies 66-8
  history of 64-6
Children of God, Australia 87
Christianity 15, 20, 25, 69, 132
Civic Daycare Centre case 82

Cleveland case 115-8, 122-3
Cooperites 91
Counselling, recall in 50-1
Country Walk Babysitting Service case 78-80
Courtroom procedures 23, 141-2
Credibility 52-3
Custody cases 96-102

Definitions of sexual abuse 54-61
  difficulties in 59-61
  legal 55-6
  retrospective 58-9
  social 56-7
  sociological 58
Diagnosis of child sexual abuse 140
Distortion of memory 41-9
  by current beliefs and feelings 45
  by interviewer expectations 43-4
  by post-event misinformation 42-3
  by sharing memory with others 44-5
  by thinking, writing about and discussing memory 44
  by time 42
  confusion of dream or fantasy with memory of real event 44-5
Disclosure interviews 73, 77-82, 140
Dolls, anatomically correct 36, 45, 47, 79, 98-100, 140
Double standard 30-1
Dualism 132

Education, issues regarding 34, 104, 139-40
England
  cases in 24, 85-6, 103, 114, 117-8, 122
  laws in 55-7, 65

sexual abuse issues in 64, 70, 115
126

False allegations 40, 96-107, 140
  emotional payoff from 104-5
  financial gains from 105-6
  pressure from other people causing
    103-4
  teenage retribution 102-3
Feminism 25, 27-32, 36, 130, 135
Forgiveness 131-4
France
  cases in 86
  sexual abuse issues in 65

Germany, cases in 69-70, 86, 92
Gonorrhoea 21, 28, 80
Greece, classical era 20, 33, 64, 83,
  132

HELP Sexual Assault Centre 6-8, 57,
  110
Herpes 22, 29
Holland
  cases in 24, 70, 84-5, 92
  sexual abuse issues in 64, 71
Homosexuality 19-20, 55, 67, 128
Hotlines 109-10
Hymen, measurement of 115-7, 141
Hypnosis, recall in 50-1

Iatrogenic abuse 73
Incest 34, 38, 56, 64, 70, 143
Indicators
  behavioural 22-3, 76, 140
  physical 115-8, 141
Islam 21, 30, 132

Japan, laws in 55
Jordan case 83-4

Judaism 16-7, 132

Legal issues 55-6, 144

Mandatory reporting 108, 140
Masturbation 22, 33, 68
McMartin Preschool case 77-8
Media, effects of 130, 144
Medical examination 115-8
Memory
  accuracy of 41, 43, 52
  accuracy under stress 52
  distortion of 41-9 (*see also* Distortion
    of memory)
  effects of interviewing techniques on
    46-9
  recall in counselling 50-1
  recall in hypnosis 50-1
  reconstruction 35, 41-5, 50-1, 59,
    63, 105, 107, 113, 140, 143
Middle Ages 20, 25, 33, 64-5, 83
Moral panics 29-30, 94
Multiple personality disorder 112-4
Munchausen Syndrome by Proxy 114-5

Networking 36, 119-20
New Zealand
  cases in 41, 48-9, 72, 82, 88-91, 94
    98-101, 104, 110, 113-4, 116, 123
  laws in 55-7
  sexual abuse issues in 35, 26, 38, 62
    105-6, 126, 130

Offenders
  children as 73-4
  registers of 123-5
  treatment of 38, 143-4
Orkney Islands case 85
Oude Pekela case 84-5

Subject Index

Paedophilia 70-3, 94
Parents Against INjustice (PAIN) 126
Persecution of professionals 36, 122-3, 141
Physical indicators of abuse 115-18, 141
Police procedures 141
Politics of sexuality 19-22
Prevalence of sexual abuse 37-8, 58-63
Prevention programmes 36, 97, 120-22

Reality, subjective nature of 15-18
Recovered memory *see* Memory, reconstruction
Reflex anal dilatation 116-8, 141
Registers of sex offenders 123-5
Relationships between men and women 134-6
Religion 14-7, 21, 30, 71, 83
Research findings:
    Alternative communities 86-7
    Anthropological studies 20, 66-8
    Child pornography 92-3
    Clinical judgement 51-2
    Consequences of sexual abuse 60-1
    False allegations of abuse 40, 97-8, 102-3, 107, 109
    Iatrogenic abuse 73
    Interviewing techniques 46-7
    Medical examination 115-6
    Memory 42-7, 50-1
    Neuropsychology 17
    Prevalence of abuse 56-9, 61-3
    Prevention programs 121-2
    Satanic abuse 83
    Sexual experiences of children 66-70
    Sexuality 30
    Violence 130
    Witness accuracy 52-3

Research issues 36-7, 54, 138-9
Ritualistic abuse *see* Satanic ritual abuse
Rochdale case 85-6

Satanic ritual abuse 83-6
Satanism 23-4, 75, 83-6
Sex rings 76
Sexual practices of non-Western cultures 20, 66-8
Sexual rights of children 70-3
Sexuality
    as social construct 18-9
    of children 68-70
    politics of 19-22
START sexual Abuse Centre 116
Statistics, interpretation of 61-3
Suggestibility 41, 47-9, 140
Syphilis 21, 23, 28

Treatment
    of offenders 38, 143-4
    of victims 128-37, 142-3

United States of America
    cases in 24, 77-82, 83-4, 91, 92-4, 101-3, 107, 113, 115, 122, 124
    laws in 55-7, 65, 93-4
    sexual abuse issues in 38, 46, 70-1, 104-6, 109-10, 123-4, 126

Victorian era 20-3, 33, 65-6, 68, 137
Victimisation, secondary 73
Victimology 31-2, 38, 128-30
Victims Of Child Abuse Laws (VOCAL) 126
Violence 130, 136-7

Wee Care Day Nursery case 80-2
Women's Liberation Movement 21-2, 27-32, 134-5

HV 6570 .G63 1993

Goodyear-Smith, Felicity

First do no harm